Stop Licking That

The Novaks,

I hope you enjoy this book + laugh!

[illegible]

7/2/17

Karin Mitchell

Stop Licking That

ISBN: 978-0-9986131-0-9
Library of Congress Control Number : 2017902152

Praise for Stop Licking That

There were so many moments when I thought "yep, exactly." Written by a real mom and a damn funny person. I appreciated that "Stop Licking That" got serious too. Because those moments are important and deserve attention.

~ *Ruth Hendricks, early childhood professional and mother of 2* ~

As a Mom and Psychotherapist, "Stop Licking That!" is a must have. Karin Mitchell tells the ridiculous and rash parts of parenting that are both hilariously honest and heart-wrenchingly truthful. She tells the stories that every parent can relate to without feeling an ounce of shame. It's refreshing to read about the same triumphs and disastrous fails we have all experienced on our adventure as parents. "Stop Licking That!" will absolutely be added to my shelf of must-have books!

~ *Sammy Charytoniuk, Licensed Professional Counselor and mom*~

"I laughed out loud so hard my husband came up to ask me what was the matter."

~ *Michelle Woods Pennisi, childbirth educator, doula, & mother of 2* ~

"Karin has such a way with words. Reading this brought back that my friends and I, in High School, had licking contests. The essence of the game was to lick something your competitor was not willing to lick, like the game chickin, but with bacteria, disease, and filth being the epicenter. It was pretty foul, and hilarious. Also probably an explanation for why were often ill in high school."

~ Drew Mikita (AKA Chicken Licken), Associate Professor Psychology and dog dad ~

Dedication

To my partner in crime, Rob. You're the best. But seriously, stop letting the kids eat everywhere.

Contents

Part Four:

Part Five:

PART ONE
The Identity Thief: Pregnancy

Rob: "How do you sat 'crazy' in Swedish?"

Me: "Tokig." (pronounced too-kig)

Rob: "Two kids?"

Me: "Yes."

Chapter 1

Who we are

Karin, the mom. Rob, the dad. The software that made our avatars knew that I'd look better with a mustache. In real life I have to borrow a fake one.

Stop Licking That

We have two boys. I changed their names in this book to help my chances of them still talking to me when they're older. I have also turned them into cartoons. This is only fair. They have turned me into a different-looking person too. Our children are Mars and Gomez. They are two years apart. At the writing of this book, Mars was five. And Gomez was three.

This is Mars

And this is Gomez with a roller in his hair

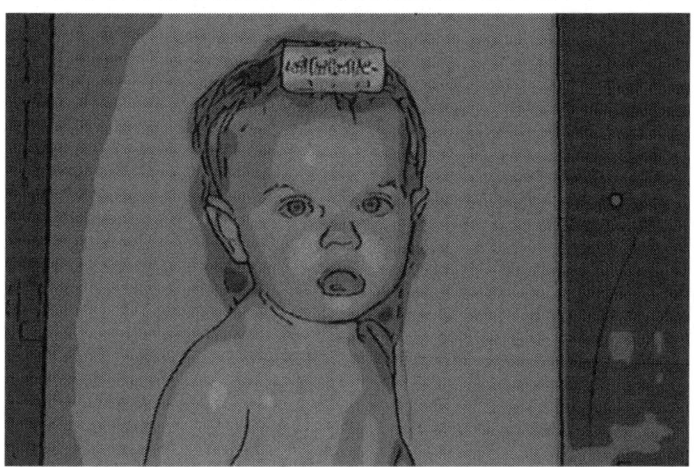

When I was pregnant, all my maternity clothes were black. Clearly being pregnant made me a ninja.

Chapter 2

Mix 'N Match Me

Before my actual children, I had decided exactly how awesome my parenting identity would be. I'd be great at it. In fact, I would be far better than I'd ever been at being a single adult, and I'd rocked that. I was ready to let go of my single life. I planned to simply build on the momentum that had been the last few years of adulthood. I'd learned to drop cliffs on skis, made the best friends you could sass around with (but beware, they cheat at cards), traveled the world, and finally met and married my husband. I truly thought I could ride this momentum like a wave for the rest of my life. I was ready to have kids.

I'd decided that my kids would get all my best traits: a strong sense of self; creativity; my love of music & art & story; and they'd obviously have fantastic taste in music. They would never, ever know anything about "Baby Beluga" because they'd be so busy learning all the words to every Gorillaz and Beastie Boys song. I would never yell or spank or say something stupid like "stupid." I was going to be incredible and perfect in every way. That was my plan. That was my identity. And so I got pregnant.

Pregnancy starts all exciting with the peeing on the stick and the idea of it and then bam! You go to the OBGYN, or as I prefer to call her, the twatdoc. And you've seen a million shows where the doctor comes in and squirts some goop on a sticky-outie mommy belly and then comes the ultrasound wand and the image of her baby. Everyone's choked up as the camera filter goes all blurry and soft. But in real life, that first visit, that first ultrasound?

It was more like...

"You'll need to remove your clothes below the waist. You can cover up with this." They told me this in the same monotone they always had at every prior non-pregnant twatdoc visit. They handed me the usual folded up, baby blue paper napkin, the same one I'd had at every appointment of my entire adult life. Then, as a consolation before leaving the room, they added, "You can leave your shirt and bra on."

Oh, jeez, thanks eversomuch.

Then I sat feeling like an idiot, waiting for the doctor. A friend told me once that the nurse at her twatdoc had told her that all women fold their clothes up neatly without their underwear showing. Seemingly we'd all universally received a shameful memo about hiding our whorish undies and looking tidy. I had also received the message and done the careful folding, but with this news, changed my routine immediately. From that moment on, I refused. All women, my foot! I'd show her...or them, or the cosmos...or someone. From then on, every visit, I've balled up my clothes however they came off and shoved them under a chair. They remain in their devil-may-care, take-that position, until the punishment of stirrups is over. Every time. Take that, someone!

But what's always struck me as odd about the indeterminate wait time between taking your clothes off and the doctor coming in is that you sit naked with a paper blanket on your bottom half, looking normal and reading a book on the top half. It always made me feel like one of those children's flip flap books with the animal parts. You know, where you turn the page and get an ostrich's feet and a giraffe head? I felt like that.

They did that polite door knock, and then came in and asked soft-voiced, "Ready?"

"Uh huh." But I was not ready. I was, in fact, unprepared for the next part and I know I'm not alone in my surprise.

"What the what? What's happening? Doesn't that go on my belly?"

The doctor barely coughed into her elbow and explained, "Oh, no. The first is an 'internal' ultrasound."

The first ultrasound isn't like on TV and movies. It's a dildo with a condom and an absurd amount of lube and they shove that wand right in your vagina.

It is not a sexy moment between you and the twatdoc. But screaming about it doesn't exactly fit into your perfect mom identity, so you just go "Oh, that's okay."

It's not okay. It's annoying. Which is mostly how real pregnancy is. Annoying.

Pregnancy goes on and on and on and on and you get to see the twat-doc way more often than you ever thought of when you pictured your pastel pregnancy full of serene contemplative moments straight out of a pottery barn nursery. Cue the tinkling nursery music.

It's not *at all* like the pottery barn nursery filled with tinkling music. I mean, you *do* tinkle a lot. And if you're like me, you probably sing songs to yourself, but there's not this serene, saintly, calm thing you imagine. There are varicose veins in your ass. That's what a hemorrhoid is. Who needed to know that? I'm sure I didn't, but I can't unlearn it. So I'm telling you. You can also get skin tags, which if they happen in the right place on your boob are like an extra nipple. Also, occasionally some poor woman gets an *actual* extra nipple out of pregnancy. And if you think an extra nipple doesn't impact your identity, you are ever-lovin' nuts. Even if you don't get an extra nipple, you get something. Maybe you get a pubis that pops from all the extra Relaxin hormone in your system, and a belly that you swing into things all the time, and then feel like an idiot for bonking your baby into a counter, even if it is protected in utero. All that's to say, well...pregnancy's a shift. Where I used to have my stomach not bonk into things, now it was like a giant extra appendage. Where I used to have strangers glare at me and say things like "Hey Jerkface, that's my parking spot," now suddenly strangers cocked their heads and smiled in an extra kind way. I was used to apologizing for my existence, so this new niceness was difficult to interpret. Men tipped their caps, women opened doors, and people talked to me constantly. It was weird.

Being pregnant is a lot like going to a museum or monument you wanted to see, but you didn't want to stay for long. In fact, you walked in with a plan in mind for leaving soonish but then someone exclaimed how moving this installment/sculpture/tapestry/ historic monument is and how under-appreciated it is and so you felt obligated to stay there and feign homage and fascination for a loooonnng time. And don't get me wrong, at the end you really are glad you saw it but you only needed an hour tops. Not the four hours it turned into.

But at least with going to see Mount Rushmore or going to the Alamo, at the end you had a giant ice cream cone. Because at the end of the Pregnant Museum, instead of having an ice cream beneath the noses of the four most prominent US presidents, you have labor. For like 20 hours. Beneath the noses of some combination of family, friends, nurses, midwives, doctors, lawyers, orderlies, and plumbers. And during the labor, you didn't even care or notice those noses in your business.

When you're pregnant there are near-constant visits to the twatdoc. And the flip flap version of your body gets more and more distorted with each visit. They just flip the pages week by week. Suddenly, one week my face was mine, but then someone had flipped the middle page to these giant boobs and then there was this big ole belly and the bottom part was me again. Mix 'n match ME! Except, I think toward the end, someone might have even switched the feet pages to give me someone else's. I might've had hooves. I wouldn't know though. I couldn't see what was going on down there. Which was probably for the best.

I hated being pregnant. I love my kids and they were totally worth it, and like the museum, I'm glad I had the experience. It was amazing to feel a baby move inside my belly. It was cool and I'm glad I did it but

I definitely didn't enjoy multiple months of my life where tying my shoes and picking up items I dropped felt *so* hard. I really could have had a one-hour pregnancy experience of giant boobs and feeling the baby move, and then just had ice cream. But that's not how it works, or so they tell me. I did it twice just to be sure. It was a long, long, flip flap museum the second time too.

Pregnancy the second time was a special challenge in that my existing kid climbed all over me and wanted to put temporary tattoos on his unborn sibling constantly. And this meant my belly was out constantly. So the second time my flip flap book included a naked belly with the pants folded down and temporary tattoos. This also meant I folded down that belly band thing on my pants that screamed SEXY MAMA but really held my pants up. So my pants would be falling off. And then it was like I was an old, fat plumber with body parts sticking out but without the benefit of cheap beer. Add that to your flip flap book. No beer, plus plumbing. No way to plumbing. Plumbing would have been so, so hard. Way too hard, as it would have involved getting down on the floor to do the plumbing and then doing wild contortions like getting back up again. And my pants falling off. Again, no beer. Or wine. Or margaritas or vodka or whiskey. Instead, I flipped the piece of the page that should've been holding a drink, and in place of a globular glass tumbler of awesome, my hand held my pants. Sexy. New. Me.

Just like the ultrasound, the whole process seems pretty simple and awesome from the outside. Until your identity is the one turned flopsy and strange, it seems like you'd just pee on a stick, wait and enjoy ice cream and not holding your tummy in and then reap the benefits of a beautiful cherubic baby. But like the rest of parenthood, the challenges are simple, yet hard to surmount. The first challenge is a new identity, AKA pregnancy. Find my identity in a bellyband? Oh boy.

I wonder if I could learn to read braille. Then I wonder if I'd be tempted to read over someone's shoulder. That leads to me wondering if some blind person would whack me with their cane for reading over a person's shoulder. I know *I* would. I'd be a mean blind girl.

Chapter 3

Swimming While Pregnant

I pushed open the glass door to a tourist shop and stepped into the relief of air conditioning. The door jingled, announcing our entrance and a short, stout man with obviously dyed black hair looked up and greeted us.

"Hi there," I said, smiling in gratitude for air conditioning, as the door shut behind my husband. "I saw the flyers in your window and I was wondering about going ziplining."

The man glanced down at my belly.

"I think that is not allowed," he said, avoiding eye contact.

I blinked and waited then asked, "Why *can't* I go zip-lining?"

The tour seller answered, "Because." He gestured at my obviously pregnant belly which was HUGE and twitching with a baby foot. You could probably make out the baby's toe prints. Probably.

I shrugged. "What?" I feigned dumb and refused to confess my unprotected sex.

The tour seller, suddenly unsure of himself and visibly uncomfortable asked, "You're pregnant?" His accent was thick and desperate. If an accent could sweat, his did. He waited for the confirmation but I just stared and blinked.

Rob felt sorry for the guy, though, so he told him, "Yes, she's pregnant. She likes to tease people. She just thinks it's fun to ask if she can go ziplining." I love him because he never once said "sorry about my crazy wife."

I have always loved messing with people and pregnancy was no different. Well, except people really expected you to be a nice, saintly sort of woman while pregnant, and so they were more-than-the-usual-amount of surprised to be teased. I know because I did it more than once on this trip.

One of the weirdest parts of pregnancy for me was the slow-motion saint impression that people seem to think is pregnancy and women. Suddenly, you're nice and nurturing and glowing and golden and globular. After years of any sexual look or behavior you've shown being treated like actual prostitution, now sex has made you glow. Remember the memo about the filth that is a woman's underwear? Chuck it out the window during pregnancy. Seriously, you're wearing the evidence of unprotected sex, and somehow this makes everyone think you've become a saint. Slowly.

On our trip to Belize, this was evident whenever I went into the tourist shops and teased about going caving or ziplining. People hollered their prediction of the gender of the unborn baby across streets and were generally surprised at my existence.

We went to Belize while awaiting our first baby. It was a fabulous idea. We went because we knew it would be our last chance for a trip like that. We were a teacher and a social worker; our salaries combined to mean we made 11 cents over what we needed to live and eat every month, so we were unlikely to get to go to Belize again for a long time. That and I was huge and hot all the time and it sounded nice to leave the mountains and go somewhere to swim a lot outside. So we went to Belize. Ah...I like to say "Belize." It makes me feel like pre-baby me...Belize...zzz.

At this point, I thought I loved being pregnant. I liked people being nice to me. I had just started feeling the baby move and that was fascinating. So I thought I liked pregnancy. Did I mind that I was moving more slowly every day and that my feet were beginning to swell?

Sure, but people were nice to me. Did I like that no one expected me to mess with them anymore? Yes, yes I did. It added a heap to the shock value when I still *did* mess with them. But I didn't like how hard it was to climb to the top of a temple at dawn, or how hot I was, and apparently, I'd forgotten that my body used to be able to do more than swim laps at the same rate as a whale. And not a regular whale either. That'd be badass; I'd be a giant swimming badass. But no, No, NO. I did not feel like a badass. No, I felt like a dolphin midway through calving a whale. Uncomfortable, right? Yup, and like something was happening to change me fundamentally and I would maybe rip apart and never be myself again. And I liked being me. So I tried to remind myself of what it was like.

I needed to feel like myself. *All* myself instead of just a section. No parts whale. No parts plumber. No flipped pages. No torn pieces. All parts Karin. So I tried things to feel like myself. I bought pretty heels that I never wore and a purse that I never carried. These things would surely allow me to feel normal and like myself, right? Again, no.

Especially because I don't really care about purses or shoes. Those were just in sections of my body I thought wouldn't grow, so they seemed like a good, practical choice. But I'm not a shoe or purse girl. At least three times a week, I accidentally wear my flipflops to work because I forget to change out of my "houseshoes" AKA flipflops and into professional foot ware. I've been carrying a castoff purse a friend gave me for about three years now. When it rips off my shoulder, I'll pin it back together to avoid having to get a different purse. Purses and shoes are not the answer for me, but they were worth a try. What really worked to make me feel like myself was swimming. It felt good. So, so good.

I've always loved to swim but I love it at a brand-new level when I'm hot and huge.

At the end of my second pregnancy, I told Rob that at some point he would hear from the police that I was at our recreation center refusing to get out of the pool.

"Uh sir, can you please come and pick up your wife? She's in the recreation center pool and she says she won't get out until the baby comes. It's been five hours. We're not getting anywhere with her. We were hoping you could help us out? Uh, please?"

This is what I fantasized about while swimming slowly back and forth, counting the minutes I had left of weightlessness. I'm sure the cops have to be nice to slow, saintly pregnant ladies. It's in the rules.

I swam often with both pregnancies. Obviously, the ocean in Belize was the best. But I also loved the feel of moving through a swimming pool or the several lakes and ponds I managed to plop myself into in my home state. I had so much blood pumping, my body felt like the inside of a sauna. But in the pool there was that cool, cool water. And the relief from gravity. Moving was easy. It was wonderful.

One day toward the end of pregnancy, I was swimming slowly back and forth at my local recreation center pool when a guy interrupted me.

"Can I split the lane with you?"

I had seen him preparing to enter. He sat on the white plastic bench at the end of the lanes and removed his prosthetic leg slowly. He took many steps to his process, waiting and watching to see if anyone was about to finish up. The lanes were full. No one was finishing. Eventually, he gave up and looked for the weakest link to ask to share that poor sucker's lane. It was clearly me. I was the slow sucker. Saintly, round.

"Ok, but you have to race me for it." The fact that I tried to make a man with a prosthesis race me for my lane also made me feel normal. There's no saint in that. Slow or not.

Things like that got me through pregnancy. I needed an occasional, irreverent distraction. I needed to be me: not slow, fast and risky but irreverent, silly, and slightly strange. But I should have known that I was going through actual changes that would impact my identity. They were slow, but they were there. I can't say I really accepted them. Fought them? Yes. Allowed them...begrudgingly. Accepted them...meh, not really.

I dislike the word vagina. I'm thinking of replacing it with vagrant. Although that makes my vagina sound homeless and drunk. Get that vagrant off my lawn! Get that grass off my vagrant? Nevermind. I probably shouldn't mess with the current terminology.

Chapter 4

OMG, Is This Birth Going to Rip Me to Pieces?

The first time I met my editor I was pregnant with my second son. She and I were in a master's class together. As I entered the room, someone in the class asked, "How far along are you?"

I answered, "Not as far as you think."

That was months before I gave birth. I didn't get more graceful at handling these conversations.

The end of pregnancy is for the birds. There's nothing to say to anyone except "I'm sick of being pregnant" and, "We're ready any time" and, dejectedly, "I can't wait for this to be over." By the end, there's no more faking cheer for a stranger. There's glaring and staring into space. Also, drooling. I drooled a lot in my pregnant, oft-interrupted sleep.

By the end of pregnancy with my first, the sweet and friendly interest of strangers had long lost its luster. I was sick to death of mustering a response to: When's your due date/how far are you/are you having a boy or a girl/I bet you're sick of this/what hospital are you going to? I was always sick of "are you having twins?" That was infuriating every single time. Never, ever, EVER ask someone that unless you see four feet sticking out of her belly and then for heaven's sake just look the other way. I did not have twins. I just made the fetal version of an Olympic-sized swimming pool with the ingredients available to me at the time: Healthy nutrients, a lot of water, and an especially stretchy uterus. In short, I was 76 pounds up and HUGE by the time I had my first baby, but I sure was crafty with ingredients. Even my face was huge.

There's something misleadingly innocuous about a Tuesday. On the Tuesday after Labor Day in 2010, I awoke to overwhelming pains. I endured three contractions which had felt very close together before I awoke my husband, Rob. We timed the contractions. They doubled me over, lasted 30 seconds each, and happened every five minutes. It was time to call the midwife.

I had my children at home in serene beauty with a goddess/midwife. Okay, maybe this isn't exactly true, but that's how I'd pictured it. I'd grown up with arguably the most unrealistic idea of birth you can have. My aunt had given birth at home, and it had been beautiful and peaceful and the baby had not even cried. My mom happened by just in time to cut the cord. My aunt then put a lasagna in the oven and everyone came down to dinner. I'm not kidding. This is what really happened.

Since I wanted to do everything just like this woman who was always larger than life to me, I gave birth at home. I did not do this easily. I did not want anyone but my husband near me. I did not serve lasagna.

On that Tuesday at 2 a.m., the midwife instructed my husband to call her back when a) the contractions got more intense, b) they were 3 minutes apart, or c) they were 60 seconds long.

An hour after the first phone call, Rob timed a pair of contractions.

Me, panting: How long? How far apart?

Rob: 3 minutes 10 seconds apart. 50 seconds long.

Me: I think we better call her. They're more intense and 3 minutes apart.

Rob: I don't know...she said 3 minutes apart and they're 3 minutes, ten seconds apart.

Me: CALL HER!

I was glad we didn't have to go anywhere. I was anxious for the midwife and her assistant to arrive. I knew their expertise would comfort me and that they would take over some of the logistics so that Rob could focus all his attention on helping me.

Rob called and I settled back in my bed to try to relax until they got there. They got there and told me to try to rest. Back to "resting." They thought I was sleeping until about 8 a.m. I assure you, I was not. For some strange reason, I thought I should get up and interact with them once 8 o'clock hit. Like, I was hosting them and it was improper for me to sleep in so late with guests to serve a baby up for! I should have stayed with the faking asleep thing. Instead, I got up and started moving around. Things got more intense then. As in, this was, to this day, the one time I thought "I might die." And that thought didn't seem so bad.

It's hard to describe the change to your state of consciousness during birth. During contractions, I was aware of contractions. I was aware of my keen hatred of the more chipper and uplifting of the two midwives. I heard the midwife I liked, the one who had more experience and had actually given birth, count down after the crest of each contraction. I was aware that Rob was next to me and I cleaved to him with my life. He did not let me down. What he actually did was strategically listen to each of the midwives' comments. If I reacted favorably, he repeated the comment. It was a very effective strategy. He said the right thing every time.

What I was not aware of was that my dog and cat lurked over my shoulders. I was not aware of the sun changing angles and time passing. It was like a piece of my consciousness was in a balloon elsewhere. And that was the piece that cared if anyone saw me naked. I usually cared. But during labor, I absolutely didn't. I could not wear clothes. It was weird.

I was keenly aware at three points during labor when I yelled at someone:

1. The midwife checked my cervix and there was a lip of cervix holding back the baby. She moved it. It hurt like crazy and I did not hide that. I screamed "GET YOUR FINGER OUT OF MY F#CKING TWAT." The other midwife choked back a laugh.
2. I was aware of the music of Erykah Badu, Toots and the Maytals, and Chopin's Nocturnes. Those were helpful. But then, the music changed. Rob had done this. He clicked the wrong thing, but then didn't know what to do when he realized his mistake. When not in labor, I can be a royal snob about music I don't like. During birth...well, it's safe to assume my senses were heightened and the consequences could be dire. I was unaware of Rob's predicament. He vacillated between leaving my side, which he knew I would not like, or letting the unfavorable music play, which he knew I would not like. He deliberated too long and some 70's progressive rock synthesizers came on. "WHAT THE EFF IS THIS?" To this day, my husband thinks if he'd let that song go on any longer, I'd have pulled him into the birthing tub and drowned him. But everyone scrambled to remedy the situation.
3. My dog licked me. I yelled at him to stop. I should have known then that this was the beginning of years and years of the indigents of my household licking things and my inability to actually stop them.

But aside from those three moments, a big part of consciousness was in the balloon, floating through some 'elsewhere'. Suddenly, it came time, my body forcefully told me so and I pushed. I made it through contraction after contraction. Listening to Rob's voice, listening to Chopin, going somewhere far but keeping my feet in the now because I just had no other choice.

I tried many positions. I pushed in the birth tub. Then I got out and was on the toilet but the idea of telling your baby later, "sorry I dropped you in a toilet for your first moment in this world...No, no, that birthmark would have been on your head either way. I swear."

So, I got off the toilet. I squatted in the bedroom. I got tired doing that on account of how I weighed a thousand freaking pounds. I hung from a sheet that was held up by the doorway somehow. Rob attempted to hold my massive body up so I could hang from his arms. This was not sustainable.

I had, by this time, managed to push hard enough to feel a horrible, terrifying burning sensation no one had bothered to warn me of. It was called the "Ring of Fire."

"Ring of Fire" up to this point in my life had meant the go-home-already-drunkie song from my favorite dive bar. It came on just before the lights came on and we all stumbled home. But my life was in process of changing massively and "Ring of Fire" was trying to alert me to that. Since I was unaware that a burning sensation was normal and not the sign that my body was about to rip in half, I stopped when I felt it. It's the sort of sensation that normally means, "Uh oh. Nope. Don't do that."

A chipper voice reported, "You can reach down and feel your baby's head." She had not long before told me that I could be having fun and dancing. I kid you not.

"I hate you! What the what? Who wants to touch a slimy baby head in the Ring of Fire that is my ripping-apart vulva? Gross!" I thought this but did not actually say anything. I just shook my head vigorously and attempted to breathe through what was happening.

So then I lay on the bed on my side with my foot pushing against the tiny chipper midwife who told me I could have fun and dance my way through labor. The one who weighed about as much as I'd gained. I pictured my giantess mighty legs pushing against her tiny frame and launching her into the birthing tub. HEAVE. Splash! Instead, my amniotic sac ruptured like a balloon and wet her entire front. HA! She totally deserved it.

I did not have a concept of time. But I did have a sense that the midwives wanted to see the baby come out. That it was maybe taking longer than they really liked. The problem was the contraction part where I could push and really use the contraction to push wasn't lasting long enough to push the baby out. So then I was pushing past the end of the contraction. And this threatened to rip me to pieces in a way that would maybe mean I would never, ever enjoy sex again. Didn't I mention earlier how I'd rocked adulthood? I really enjoyed sex. It was the best part of adulthood. I wanted to do it again someday with zero in utero guests.

Yet, there came a point where I was afraid of what could happen if getting the baby out took too long. The baby was more important than my future sex life. Plus, I really, really wanted to leave the pregnant museum and go back to being me. Little did I know that the woman I'd been was long gone.

I dug in. I became determined to push the dang thing out, contraction help or no. I pushed and felt myself ripping and burning. It stung and felt wrong. They assured me I just had to push through it. So I pushed more.

I pushed from the good point in the contraction, past it, after it, until finally, I felt so much tearing and this giant slimy thing come out.

And it was so, so gross. Like, way grosser than varicose veins in your ass.

They put the baby on my chest, slimy and wet. Rob caught a glimpse. A boy. And that boy immediately peed on me. This is how our in-person relationship began.

I looked down at his face and could not believe how perfect, how beautiful, how golden, how amazing he was. I don't think most babies are cute when they're born. And I was certain that if my own child was not cute, I would know. I would know, and when people told me he was cute, I would think, "Liar." Even more likely, I would actually say "liar."

But he was the most beautiful thing I'd ever seen. All 8 lbs, 2 oz of him. All 20 and ¾ inches of him. His hair and his tiny nails. His pooling dark eyes, and his short even breaths as he drifted to sleep. Positively stunning. Unquestionably fascinating. Life-altering.

But before taking any sort of moment, or taking a rest, the midwives were already shouting at me that I needed to give birth to the placenta.

"What the...seriously? I just got done with the grossest worst thing ever. I can't rest?"

Nope. So there was then the afterbirth to deliver. Gross. More revolting slimy-ness. But then, I thought, then I'd get rest and baby time. Life-altering, mood changing baby time.

But no. Because there was still the issue of the labia/vagina-tearing that needed to be dealt with. Onto the repairing business.

From the birth, I had a tear and some other nonsense going on. Like, a HOLE in my labia. Both midwives said they'd never seen someone get a piercing out of birth, but there it was! The prize for originality goes to? ME!

They started stitching. And I proceeded to tell a skiing story to distract myself from what was happening to the girl downstairs.

A few years prior, we'd had a beautiful powder day. I'd been on the mountain for first chair. For anyone who does not ski, let me emphasize that powder skiing is the best thing in the whole world. You float; you can try new tricks and jump off things you wouldn't otherwise, because it's soft. I once jumped off a little brick building on skis on a powder day, fell, and had zero injuries. On a powder day you hear men and women in their sixties giggle like school children. It's incredibly silly and fun and the whole vibe of the mountain is one of Christmas morning. People rush to play and frolic and goof around.

On this particular powder day, I had been with some friends who I especially enjoyed skiing with, and we headed for some rocks they knew of to jump off.

I was game to hit the big rock, a 15-20 foot drop. I pointed my skis and hit it with confidence. Which usually means I land it.

But this time, not so.

I don't know if my ski bindings weren't set to a high enough setting to keep me in or if I whacked something small in the landing or what, but one ski immediately ejected. The other stayed on.

One foot went through the snow. The other stayed on. Which meant that one ski's binding made a little go for my twat. It literally tried to fuck me. Probably about two inches to the left though. I slammed through the snow with 20 feet of free fall momentum with my lady bits taking the impact against a ski binding. It didn't feel any too hot.

I took a minute to collect myself. But then I got up, got my gear back on, and enjoyed the rest of the day. But my little girl swelled herself a goose egg that lasted for weeks.

So I told this story thinking that it would make me think of things I made it through just fine and distract me with thoughts of powder skiing and by the time I was done with the story, I'd also be done with the stitches.

Except when I finished, I realized the midwife had stopped stitching to listen. Dangit.

"Oh, I'm not telling any more stories. You've got reparations to make." I heckled her through the entire stitching.

"You're not making me all frankencrotch down there, are you?" and "BALLS! Did you just sew googly eyeballs into my snatch?" and comments to that effect.

To sum up: I had a boy. He's amazing and smart and beautiful. The second time I gave birth, it was the serene scene the hippies and aunties tell you about, minus lasagna. My midwife made me mac n cheese. I got another boy. He came out in one push. His amniotic sac never burst. He is beautiful and wonderful in ways that are the same and ways that are different from his brother.

I ripped myself to pieces that first time. I have since put myself back together artfully and better than ever. But I'm not the same. The pieces of me are there, plus a heap of new ones. I'm still goofy. I'll make someone with a prosthetic leg race me in the pool. And yet...I'll never be the me that I was before my children again. It's at once simple to describe and difficult to live. That's what babies do to you. They shred your identity into paper scraps of what you thought was you and make a new version. Children forever alter the landscape of every part of your life, and even if it's weird, the new version you make of yourself is a mosaic of awesome. But it's messy. In case you're still worried, I do not have googly eyes or a piercing in my labia.

PART TWO
I Got My Butt Kicked By A Baby

Why haven't more people written love songs to their coffee pots?

Screw it, I'll write one. (To the tune of "You Are My Sunshine")

You are my coffee, my only coffee.
You make me conscious, when skies are gray.
You'll never know, dear, how much I need you...
Please don't take my coffee away.

Chapter 5

Counting to Three is So Hard

If I thought pregnancy and birth were butt-kicking, and they were, it was mainly in preparation for how much not sleeping would wear me down.

Mars was a normal newborn. He fell asleep easily and slept wherever we were. He woke up every few hours to nurse and gradually those hours spread out and he woke less often. At six weeks, he'd sleep a six-hour stretch. The unfortunate thing about that stretch was that it started at 6:00 p.m. Then after he got up at midnight, he woke up every two hours. But he was only a few weeks old and so we waited, knowing this stage was temporary and normal.

To get myself a good stretch of sleep, I started going to bed at 8:00 p.m. That way I got four hours straight and then was up every two hours after midnight. But at six weeks postpartum, my body was like an Inuit using a whale, instead of burning blubber for heat, my body was burning sleep. It used every minute and I felt refreshed easily.

As I got more sleep in longer stretches, my body was like, "Oh thank Christ. I needed that." And then it staunchly refused to put up with that two-hour nonsense anymore.

So Mars extended his sleep and it seemed like he was going to learn to sleep through the night easily in time. But then at the fill-in-the-blank-month sleep regression, things took a turn and Mars stopped the longer stretch and started waking up every two hours. I stayed home with Mars for his first three months, then my husband stayed home with him for the next three. This somehow totaled four years of not sleeping for any of us when you add it up.

By four months, I was at work full time, doing child welfare. I'd come home from work so excited to see my happy, normal family, and then pass out promptly at 7 p.m., only to be woken up all night long. I'd somehow pump in the morning to leave milk for baby Mars for the day, shower, and attempt to make it out the door in one piece for work.

The next day at work would go something like this.

Cheerful coworker: "How are you?"

Zombie Me would respond, "I'm okay." LIE. Big, fat lie.

"Is that ballpoint pen on your forehead?"

"No."

I licked my finger and started wiping it off only to realize that I should not have just licked my own forehead like a cat while pretending to be a professional. I shook it off like a cat who falls over and pretends it never happened. Good job, me!

"Hey, Karin. Uh, I think your shirt is on inside out…"

"Oops."

And off I went to the bathroom to switch that around.

In the bathroom, I discovered that I had a Tuesday sock and a Wednesday sock on which meant the logical conclusion was that it was, in fact, Thursday. I also had my underwear on inside out. I rearranged my clothing only to find that my shirt had milk and spit-up on it. Back to inside out then.

I'd somehow complete my work day and return home to redo it all again.

The next day, I drove all the way to work sitting on Legos and didn't even notice. Because I'm Zen like that. Also, I realized that the word "crockpot" which I misread as "cockpit" was written on the back of my hand in blue ink and that's weird because I usually wash my hands so much and so hard that I literally wash my own skin off and have to sleep with ointment and gloves on to regrow my hands. But when I read it, I thought, "Was I making a joke about a cockpit on my hand?" Because cockpit is a funny word. What are we talking about again?

Mars was four months old so we thought he should extend his sleep longer than two hours at a stretch. He'd previously proved that he could do it. The doctor said he weighed enough to do it. She took one glance at us and correctly sized us up as too weak to force a baby to sleep. I could see it in her face. She told us he could cry and that we needed to sleep and he did too. But we are suckers. I nursed him to sleep and tried to stay sane.

In fairness, if you spend your days worrying about the safety and welfare of babies, it's hard to go home and put on a tough front to a baby. Plus, I was looking at problems with attachment in human form on a daily basis. Nothing was more important to me than the basis for healthy attachment, which is responding to a baby's needs. The baby cried, and I'd rush to him as the one baby I could really and actually protect.

But dang, I was tired. It was time to try SOMETHING. The doctor said it was okay to let him cry some but there was no way I could handle that.

I read about other options. We tried Rob giving the first feeding. I'd pump a bottle before going to sleep and then Rob could feed it to Mars while I slept so that I could get a long enough stretch to maintain some semblance of sanity. Then I'd get up for the later wakings. This helped a little but really Mars just woke up more often because he sensed that I still existed and wanted to know where.

This was not sustainable.

I slept with a stuffed animal in my shirt for four days and tried to convince him to take it as a "transitional object." This approach gives the parent the mythical idea that there is an answer. It's not true. This stage in child rearing is all about lying to yourself.

"If I sleep with this stuffy, it will smell like me and Mars will sleep with it and then he'll wake up and smell me and attach to it and he won't need to wake me up. This will allow me to sleep through the night." Lies, lies, all lies.

We tried other things too. We tried not giving Mars milk when he woke up. We tried giving him water (offensive) or soothing with only a pacifier (doable as long as you don't mind sleeping in 15 minute increments).

By the time Mars was six months old and my husband was then back at work and we were both trying to get out the door and complete the insanity that was our days, we could take it no more.

By then it was March. Signs of how on top of it I was included the day when I remembered to shave all of both of my legs. Not just one, not just the top of one, not just the bottom of another, but remembered both legs – top and bottom. But don't worry, I left the specks of nail polish from before Christmas. I also finally took the Christmas tree down. Because that's what you do in March.

It had been utterly exhausting. I totally understand how sleep deprivation is used as a form of torture. The things I find most annoying about parenting are cutting infants' fingernails and car seat installation. But the actual bad, make-you-want-to-chew-your-eyeballs-out-because-you're-too-tired-to-know-they're-not-gum crazy part of parenting is the sleep deprivation. Also, eyeballs don't come out of your head but by the time I was parenting a non-sleeping six-month-old and trying to do a difficult full time, professional job, I was no longer sure if that was really the case or not.

Maybe I could chew them...oh no, maybe I already did! Maybe that's why I feel so weird...My eyeballs are gone. Commence irrational bawling...

In our last efforts to avoid crying it out, which I was terrified would cause my child an irreparable problem with attachment, we took turns soothing him, we tried swaddling, not swaddling, and sleep sacks. We prayed to Buddha and burned dream weavers in effigy. But none of it worked and I was crying because I wasn't sure if I had eyeballs anymore or not.

"Karin, did you set this dishtowel on fire?"

"Nope." More lies. I DID set the dishtowel on fire!

I was so tired.

So we let Mars cry.

After months of trying things and talking to our doctor, Mars was getting up constantly. Since we both had to work and I was near insanity, we finally let him cry. It was physically painful for me to do, but we had tried every other systematic plan we could. So, crying it was.

Then Mars stopped waking up every two hours, and that was good, because waking every two hours was making me insane. He consolidated his sleep and instead of waking up every two hours to nurse, he only woke up once in the night. Sounds great, right?

Wrong.

He was up for *hours* at that time. He'd be up nearly every night from 1-3AM. It was so ridiculous that Rob even researched and found some farming society in history that kept this schedule. This culture went to bed with the sun and got up for a social midnight hour nightly. Maybe we could ship Mars to meet this society. We were investigating time machines.

Everyone said he would get older and grow out of it, but when? It was months. He started getting better and slept all the way through some nights and not others.

My love of coffee has grown in direct proportion to the amount of time my children have been alive and not sleeping.

I napped on weekends and chased sleep wherever I could get it. I imagined seeing progress and it seemed like we might one day be normal people. By the time he was a year, Mars began sleeping some nights all night long. He'd obviously extend this to more nights in time, and eventually all nights, right? Right? It was about to get better.

Right?

More lies.

Because then, I got pregnant again.I woke up every night for at least an hour while pregnant, both times. So I freaked out a little when I found out I was pregnant, because I had just started sleeping *some* nights *sometimes* but was still tired from the time I'd spent *not* sleeping. It was exhausting. Here's my sleep math:

No one who hasn't slept in five years is good at math.

I remember during one of Mars' hours-long waking sessions in the night, lying face down on the nursery floor and hoping he was almost done and then starting to get that loony kind of mad. I don't mean silly. I mean you start to feel like someone found your chewed-up eyeballs and put them back in backwards. And also, like maybe you could lead a mob to whoever did this person was and attack them.

"GET HIM!!"

"Ahem. Ma'am, that's a stuffed Eeyore."

Silly, audience, there's no mob following me. Or maybe I'm hallucinating… mwah! And talking to an imaginary mob and attacking a stuffed Eeyore.

Anyhoo, at the point where I was so loony I wasn't sure if there was a real mob I could lead or not, and Mars was STILL awake, I went to Rob and told him it was his turn. I attempted to stave off the hallucinations by going back to sleep. And then Rob laid on the floor and begged for his turn with the torture to be over. Mars finally gave up and went back to sleep about the time Rob was ready to lose it. It was so, so exhausting.

This period in our lives is the only time in our marriage where my husband and I have called each other names. All bets are off in the middle of the night, asshole. Daylight kiss, kiss "I love you."

The next morning I was grouchy. Rob and I fought over who would make the coffee. Then I said something like "I hate dishes I have to wash. I hate all our dishes. I even hate the dishes I don't have to wash. I hate the dishes I have to put away. And you know what else? I hate eBooks." I picked up a nearly empty syrup bottle. "I hate this bottle. I hate empty bottles of anything. I hate full bottles of anything. I hate my car keys, and I hate nouns. And verbs, too. I HATE verbs."

"Maybe you should just go take a shower."

FINE!

So I took a shower. I hated when that shower was over. Especially because when I turned the shower off, for a moment, I thought I hadn't started it yet. I was cold and didn't understand why. It was because I was standing in the shower wet, shivering and forgetting that I'd already showered and the next step was to dry off. So I turned the water back on and the water was cold. At that point, I hated cold water, cold drinks, coffee that was never strong enough, and what were we talking about again?

With pregnancy, I'm pretty sure I took 2-3 naps per day, per weekend. Mars slept more but not always. But I napped as much as a person can. I'd also quit working by then. Well, I still worked, but I didn't work full time. I substitute taught at all levels and I started tutoring in reading and writing. I tutored emerging readers all the way up through college kids. I remembered that I love to teach. Tiring, but

I napped and made it through. It was unquestionably better than working full time with trauma all day. I was clearly ill-equipped to do that. I could not separate the two parts of my life.

And then we got Gomez. Gomez, my sweet, sweet boy who loves to be held all the time. Who wants to be near me in waking and in sleep.

With Gomez, I hoped for a good sleeper. I prayed and begged for a good sleeper. I imagined that the law of averages would necessarily grant me a good sleeper.

But no.

With Gomez, I was also up all night long. And with him, there was the bonus that he would only take 20 minute naps, and only if it was silent, or he was physically touching me. He basically didn't ever want to learn to sleep anywhere but under my skin. So he'd be getting up all night long, and since I wasn't working anymore by then, I'd be getting up with him. I'd get him back to sleep just in time for Mars to wake up for a couple of hours and then I'd get Mars down, and it'd be time for Gomez to nurse again. It was as emotionally as it was physically exhausting. It was like that Whac-A-Mole game, only I was using spooning and boobs as the mallet. You, sleep. Now, you, boobwhack.

We tried lots of things to cope with the kids not sleeping. I remember a several month period of time where my survival strategy was to wake up in the morning and make breakfast and survive with the kids until 9, when Gomez went down for his morning nap. I could make it that long. Then I'd turn Sesame Street on and sleep with my head on the arm of the couch and Mars wrapped in my arms. I figured then if Mars moved, I'd wake up and protect him from whatever crazy two-year-old antics he might try. I had 20 minutes to sleep, maybe more...please let it be more? Then I just had to make it another few hours until afternoon nap. Then I'd try to get both kids to nap at the same time in the afternoon, and nap with them. After nap, we'd only have a short time in the late afternoon to play or snack or read before Rob would come home, and my hopes of him saving me could be dashed by his very real, stressful day. This was a rough time in our lives. And the biggest culprit was absolutely a lack of sleep.

I remember calling my own phone to find it, and then forgetting that's what I was doing while it was ringing. I remember thinking "when is this person going to pick up? Wait, who I am I calling?" Dumb bunny. You're calling YOURSELF! I then called a friend and couldn't stop crying. She showed up, installed my kids' car seats and took them for the day so I would stop crying and sleep. I will do anything for her for the rest of her life. Anything. I've almost volunteered to blow her husband. Almost. God, I hope she never asks me to do that.

Chapter 6

Musical Beds is Stupid

We tried lots of things to cope with the kids not sleeping. But the dumbest was the constant musical beds we played. We had three bedrooms at the time: a queen-sized bed in our room, a queen bed in the extra room, twin bunk beds, and a crib on wheels.

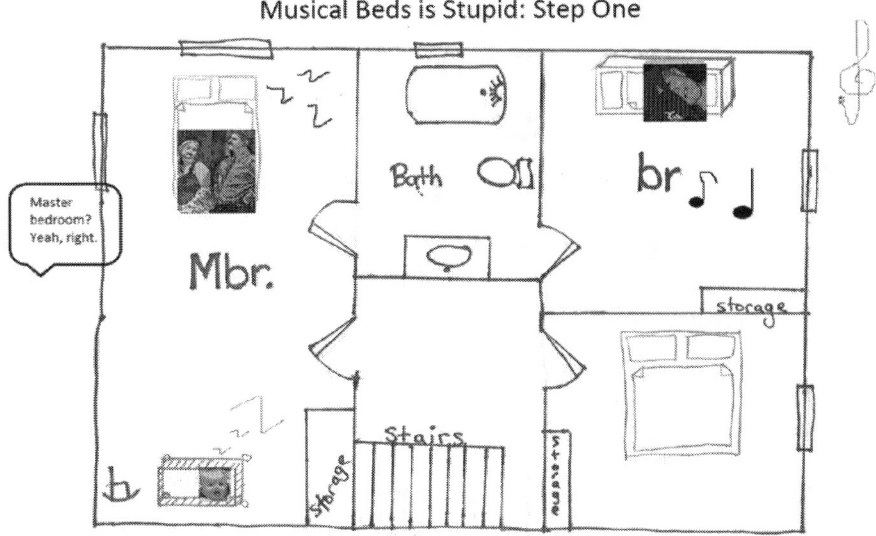

We each begin in our beds... **But then...**

Gomez, as a baby, started off sharing our room the same way we started Mars. I figured we'd transition him to sharing a room with his brother a bit later, just as we'd transitioned Mars to his own room. With Mars, I'd started with him napping in his room and when he did fine with that, we moved on to him sleeping full time in his own room.

Not so with Gomez. He wanted nothing to do with moving out of my room for any reason. Before I knew it, our doctor recommended we try moving the baby out of our room to try to get more sleep. So, we moved Gomez's crib to Mars' room. It was worth a try.

The first night we tried to let Gomez cry a little in his new shared room, he pooped AND woke Mars up. You can't let them cry if they're poopy. What are you ever supposed to do with these non-sleeping terrorists? Ahem, babies?

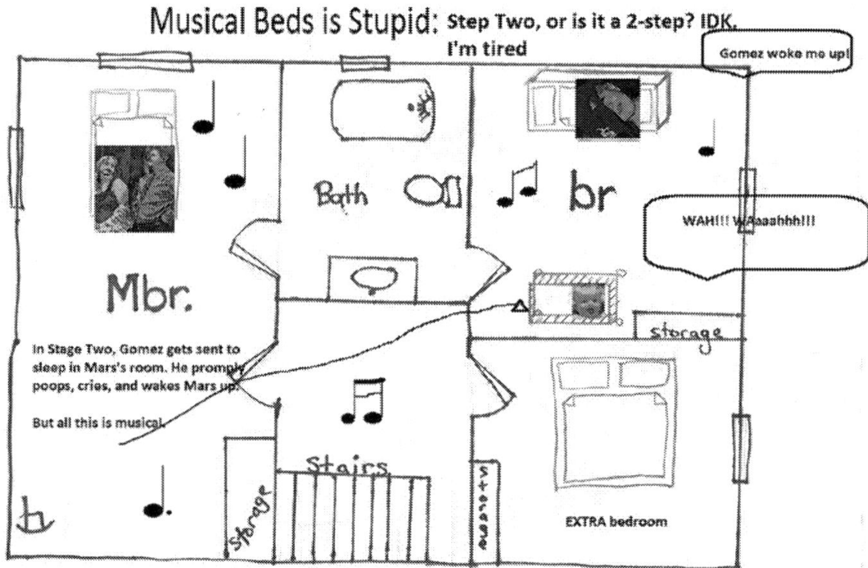

So then Gomez was getting used to the new set-up in their shared room. And after the pooping incident and dealing with getting both kids back to bed and changing a poopy diaper, we had Mars sleep in the extra bedroom. Rob and I planned to sleep in our own bed. Instead, Mars had a nightmare, and I went in with him.

Musical Beds is Stupid: **Step Three**

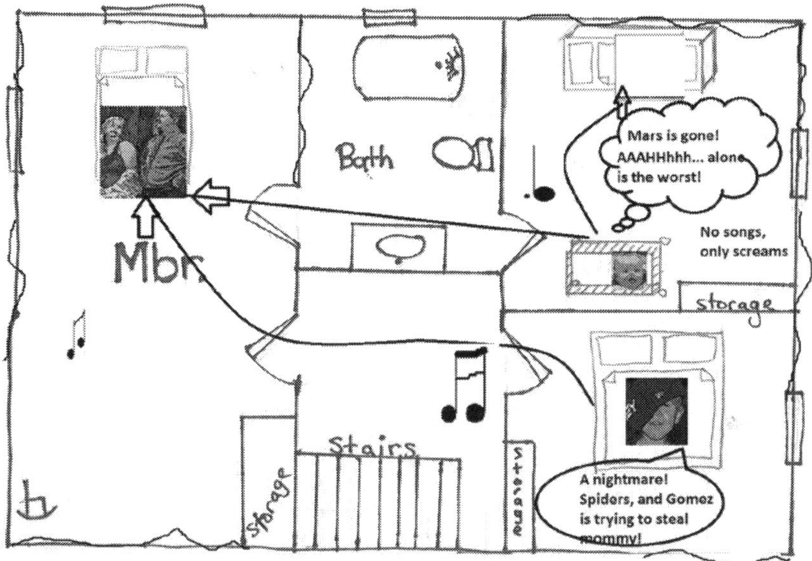

New Plan: Mars in extra bedroom. Gomez in crib getting used to new room. Ha, plan!
Music stops when Mars has nightmare
Gomez discovers he is alone, ALONE! Unsnuggled.
Music turns back on and begins to melt the walls because it's twisted and eerie.

Another night, Mars came in our room and Rob left to get better sleep in the extra bedroom. And Baby Gomez caught a whiff of missing out on mommy-snuggles, so he cried and I had to sleep with both kids in our bed. After a bit of not getting any sleep because both kids were in my bed, I went for the extra bedroom and Rob got up and slept in the crib. Okay, not that last one but still...

I forgot to add in the text of what happened in Step Five that should have been Step Four. Mars and Gomez both came in our bed and Rob left to go to the extra bedroom. Then it got dumber still.

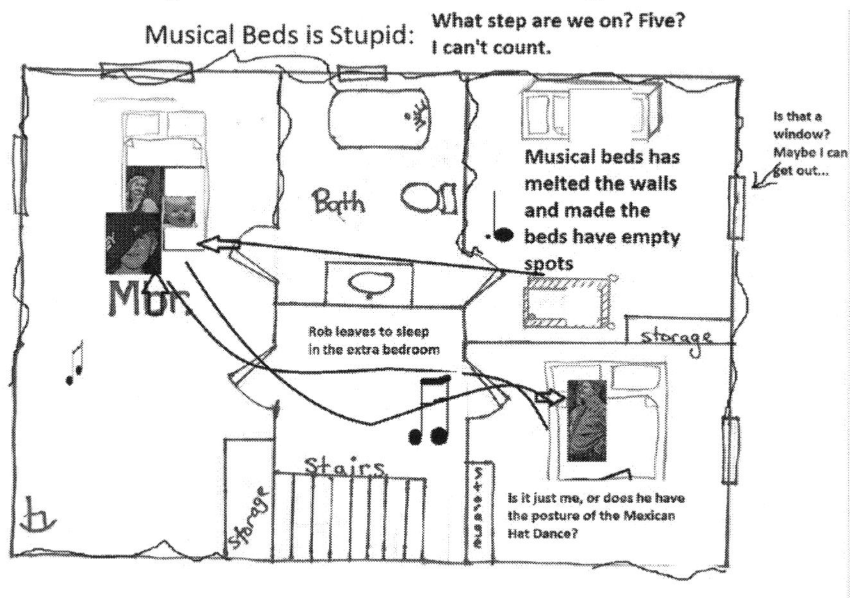

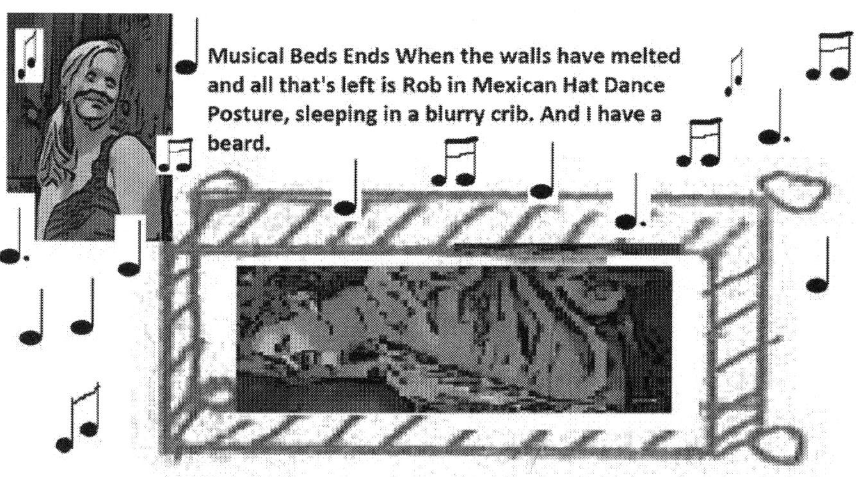

If you mess a baby up, there's no amount of salt and butter that will fix it.

Chapter 7

Why You Should Keep a Vibrator in Your Glove Compartment

I used to know this girl in high school who kept a vibrator in her glove compartment. And the only reason I thought about it such a long time later was because of a traffic jam after two airline flights with a baby in which I wished that I too kept a vibrator in my glove compartment. (I don't.) Understandably, my baby started bawling. He was good for the first flight and the layover, and the security, and the second flight. Or I've blissfully forgotten that it all sucked, who knows. Either way, those parts were over and now I finally had my baby in a car seat and we were heading home from the airport when the car stopped moving.

Baby: "What is this lack of movement? Is there a way I can make it worse? YES! SCREAMING."

As he screamed and I tried singing to him and bargaining and nothing was working, my mind searched for a novel idea.

"What if I had a vibrator in the glove compartment like that girl from high school who had way too many boyfriends?"

I'd be golden. I'd have shoved it against my baby's car seat and presto! He'd have had one of those cool vibrating baby seats. As an added bonus, if you ever decide to use this idea, you'd have to dig around your vibrator to get your registration and insurance if you got pulled over. This would add such a fabulous slant to getting pulled over.

Traffic sucked. I fantasized. Mars screamed. Eventually we made it through, and I did not get pulled over.

Speaking of getting pulled over and the police, Rob used to talk to Mars like he was a cop when he was a baby. He'd lower his voice "Sir...Sir? SIR! I'm going to need you to keep your arms inside the sleep sack."

"Sir, please take your hand out of your mouth."

"Sir, I'm going to need you to stop crying. Sir, if you'd please stop hitting yourself during diaper changes, I think we could get through this together."

Meanwhile, I took a different tack with the early stage of baby life. Since early in the baby's life, he doesn't know who moved his arms and also doesn't really understand much other than voice tone and response to his needs, I found it fun to use the sweet, mommy, sing-songy voice to talk to him about That Terrorist Baby.

That Terrorist Baby is the one I'd credit when my babies' hands would jerk in their sleep, and the jerking would wake them up. This was when they were too tiny to know they had hands. It just felt like something swatted them out of a perfectly lovely sleep.

"Oh, no," I'd say in the singy-songy mommy voice. "Did That Terrorist Baby hit you again? He woke you up, huh?"

Or "Oh no! That Terrorist Baby grabbed the kitty's tail. We better put a stop to him."

Or "Did That Terrorist Baby scratch you?"

I also extended this to when the baby would use his grab reflex to grab my hair/necklace/glasses and pull. That hurts, but it's a baby; what are you going to do? I used my imagination.

"Uh oh, That Terrorist Baby just pulled mommy's hair!"

My all-time favorite was when the baby grabbed his own wang and pulled and then cried out in desperation. I said, "Did That Terrorist Baby seriously just grab your junk? I bet that hurt, you poor baby."

I'll let you know if my kids end up with split personalities. Or if my husband gets caught with a vibrator in the glove compartment.

Cop: "Sir, is that a vibrator in your glove compartment? Sir, please step out of the car."

Rob: "No, no, Officer I swear, it's my wife's!"

Kid: "Dad, is that police officer talking to you like you're a baby?"

Rob, leaning over his shoulder would hiss at Mars before turning to look at me: "Karin, fix this."

Cop: "Ma'am?"

Me: "No way, man. Don't look at me. It was That Terrorist Baby."

And then the cops would call Special Ops.

Mars, at two: "Mom, let's pretend this is your house. The living room is your house."

Me: "Indeed. Let's pretend it's my house."

Chapter 8

I Give Up, The House is a Mess

Before I had kids, I deep-cleaned my house weekly. It was rare to find even a single stray dirty dish in my sink. I was always horrible about leaving clothes on the floor of my bedroom, but aside from that, I was very tidy. My bathroom was always clean; my kitchen was immaculate. I was pretty neurotic about it. I had a reputation among my friends for this and wore it with pride.

Now my pre-children, clean home is a distant fantasyland. In that magical place there are no dust bunnies, and I've never found two-week-old mac 'n cheese under a table. And is that mouse poop? Nope, just a very old raisin. We're still good. Raisins-turned-rock give me pause. This is a sign of how normal I still am, or so I tell myself.

In my pre-children home, I did not find multiple sticks and rocks in the living room and kitchen on a near daily basis.

My pre-children home was a land of sanitized surfaces and never having a Batman figurine embedded in my back after giving up to gravity in sheer exhaustion and passing out on the carpet. It was sparkly.

Then came the babies. I was stressed immediately after giving birth when I couldn't maintain my house. For a week after my first son was born, I couldn't even stand up straight. I had to sit on a pillow for three months. So others had to take over and help maintain it for us.

I remember all the help. I'm still grateful for all that help. People brought food and changed the baby. My husband and my mother and my father and my brother made all the meals and washed all the dishes. And the food tasted so, so good. But the piecemeal help of friends and family is nothing compared to personal neuroses. I am a better cleaner than them because I'm crazy. Or I was, before kids. Now...

My coworker recently commented that "vacuum lines are lonely." By that she meant that when we're actively connecting with our children, our houses are dirty. While I appreciated the sentiment and nodded to her face, privately I thought, "I'll lay my face in those lonely vacuum lines. My face can keep them company!"

It was stressful to let go of all that sparkalicious cleanliness. I was anxious and had trouble letting go of the control I'd previously had over my life. I'm a high-energy person, a type A person, albeit a distractible and strange one. A person who likes order and clean. I like the control it makes me feel like I have. I like the way my mind can quiet when things are clean. And how do you do that when everything's a mess all the time?

I'd look around at the mess and think "my children were sent to destroy me, to utterly unravel my whole world and leave me in a pile of exhaustion where they can then climb atop me and snuggle me into complete submission." The evidence of this? See the previous chapter on exhaustion.

A baby's mission is to wear you out so all you do is lay around paying attention to him all day, too dazed to stop any of his antics. And when he has accomplished this, he can become mobile and pull every book off your bookshelf. Then he can use the bookshelf to climb to the ceiling and swing from a light fixture. Also, he can empty every kitchen and bathroom drawer. That way if he falls, he'll probably fall on a food processor blade. Babies are terrifying. Losing control is terrifying.

We now live in a house that is far from sparkly. We live in one of the most expensive areas in the country, so we bought what was literally the only house on the market that we could get approved for. It's a Fixer-Upper. Capital F.

The top stair is about two inches tall and the bottom is about 10. There is one step that is not even the depth of a toddler's foot and they didn't bother to put padding, just carpet, atop this architectural masterpiece. Because when they built our house in 1988, they didn't have the modern luxury of a tape measure, nor basic math skills. Or maybe it was destined to house me and my mess of a family.

The first time we walked through this house, I said, "It smells like weed and paint." And those were accurate smells. The house had been rented for something like 15 years to a series of genius ski and snowboard bums who had decided to repeatedly sprayfoam-seal the garage so they could grow weed in it. They'd also had the whole house painted white because their level of chic was not to be matched. There's evidence of certain rooms once having been the color of a tangerine peel and that dancing purple California Raisin. Because what is beautiful if not purple and orange interior walls? They'd covered most of that up with a fresh coat of primer.

The result was that we bought a house with a garage door that didn't open (we've since replaced it). But the up-side was that in their rush to move, they'd left behind a massive mound of compost. Their growing soil and compost were great for setting to work on the yard, which was entirely composed of four-foot high weeds. And not of the lucrative variety. But what could be better than a lot of dirt for two boys?

Alas, we own a home, no small feat where we live. It's not all bad, this life with kids, but it does involve a significant amount of combatting clutter and mess. Compound that with our "adventurous" kids, and add still on top of that, the fun of working through the weed and paint house, which now merely smells like old carpet and whatever we made for dinner most recently, and I'm in a losing battle.

One night I got home from work and there was a hippo on the counter, a deck of UNO cards spread across the living room floor, and an empty container of lighter fluid in the dining room. The next morning, I found half of a browning apple in one corner of the shower and another half in the opposite corner, covered in shampoo. The house had been picked up completely before I'd left for work, so those items didn't blend as well as they would have on a different night. My husband loves to let the kids do whatever wherever. Eat apples in the bathtub? Why not? Use the lighter fluid container for your pretend game? Absolutely. Generally, I tend more toward the side that sets a routine around NOT doing that. If I'd been home the house would have been a different variety of a mess. I'd probably, and have on many occasions, in fact, said "you may only eat at the kitchen table."

But I've lost this battle. And anyway, it would have been a mistake to win. Do I love lighter fluid bottles in the living room? No. But I have spent time in a bubble bath with an apple now and let me tell you, an apple in the bathtub is pretty awesome. And I would have had that fight, except my husband won before I got a chance, so there are often browning apples on the tub's rim and we live in a dirty house.

Your house goes to absolute pot when you have two kids. Don't let your multi-child friends fool you at some dinner party. There are secret stashes of crap they pushed into closets at the last moment. Probably there's a garage full of crap they plopped into every laundry basket they own and shoved into the garage. Or maybe Grandma just visited for two weeks and cleaned, or they paid someone, or they're on meth and staying up all night cleaning. But they didn't do this without help. Your friends with two kids and an organized house are fooling you.

The only way I'm fooling you is if you use my house to play a real-life game of Hidden Pictures like in a Highlights magazine. I play this game constantly because there are always one or two items I need and can't find.

Not long ago, I had been looking for my glasses spray bottle to clean my eyewear. I'd thought it was just lost. On an impulse, I opened a pencil case Gomez had been playing with a lot over the previous few days to find its contents were: several bendy straws, ten or so small rocks, a AA battery, a half dozen Legos, and my glasses cleaner. Here's what I said to Gomez.

"You can't play with this. I need it to clean my glasses."

"But I need it to spray on my robot's armpits."

And how can you argue with that?

I wonder if firefighters keep their houses picked up even when they have little kids. I've tried to use the example of what would happen in a fire to convince my husband that we need to maintain a cleaner house. He's unconvinced. Then, without the husband's help with motivation, I'm often too tired to pick up before bed. So then I lay in bed worrying about the mess. The anxiety of all the hodgepodge of junk we'd trip over in a fire overcomes me and then I shop online for firefighter's boots to sleep in because we're clearly never going to get any better at this. I wonder if they make them for kids? What size do the kids wear? OMG, we're all going to die and I don't even know what size shoes the kids wear.

So, our house has gone to pot. And it's uncomfortable. There's WAY more clutter than I can handle. And by the quantity of laundry we do, you'd think there was a village in the back of my house that I'm secretly taking in the washing for in order to make ends meet. But no, this is just how much there is. The dog hasn't had a bath in three months and the bathroom floor only gets cleaned when someone drops something or I cut the kids' hair in there. But the kids and I are clean and well-fed so...my house is just a disaster for a while.

Don't stop by. Or do. It's really your call if you can handle it. I like life with my kids and it comes with the mess. Getting to a place where I can partially give in to the messiness has represented a major mental shift for me. I have to let the house be, so I can write and shower and eat and ski and do crafts with kids and read books and build forts. So if you can look past the mess, I'll share a glass of wine with you in a zebra print fort. If you can't, I understand. I can't really look past the mess either. Thus the wine, and yes, yes, I am wearing a pair of firefighter's boots.

The Disasterlands of Parenthood
Stray Crayon Marking Headquarters
The Strait of Used Band-Aids
Trench of Timeout
The Bog of Dirty Underwear
The Chasm of Couch Cushions (crumbs of indeterminate origin
Peanut Butter Smear Island
The Oasis of Lego Heads

Chapter 9

The Disasterlands of Parenting

This is what my house would look like if you made a map of it. Alas, there must be a Bermuda Triangle Zebra-Print fort but I forgot to put it in. Oh well.

Why, yes, that is a soggy rattle in my cleavage. What can I say? It's the Olympics of spring cleaning. I guess that's what happens when you only do it every four years.

Chapter 10

Pens and Knives

Once upon a time, we listed our house and sold it while raising a baby and a toddler. It was just as horrible as it sounds. I had attempted to let go of my need for control and let mess happen in our house. I drank wine and played with the children. We wore our boots and jumped in puddles. It was lovely. This seemed to be the direction I needed to go to survive and enjoy parenting. And as soon as I tried it, we had to attempt to keep the house clean. Seriously?

Inevitably the realtors called to show the house whenever it was at its worst and we showed the house approximately four thousand times that summer and then it didn't sell because the economy was terrible. So then we had to do it again the next summer.

Round 2. We still had two children, both tiny, but now even more mobile. We still had to attempt to keep the house clean. The realtors again called to show the house at its worst. We showed the house another four thousand times. Then we were successful. YAY!

Guess what we got to do then? Move. But first came packing.

I know there are so many military families who go through this repeatedly. What I always want to ask them is, "How do you move that much with children?" I bet they have advice about it. I don't.

All I know is it's terrible and eventually it's over. Do you know what packing with small children is like? It's like when you wrap presents and place them nicely under a fully decorated, lit Christmas tree and then turn your back. A toddler promptly tears all the presents open and knocks the tree over and you have to start over again. Only instead of a dozen presents, there are endless, endless boxes.

The worst part is when you're almost done and you're down to the last boxes of odds and ends. They should not be called "odds and ends" as though they DO end. I call them "pens and knives" in honor of the box I actually packed toward the end of our move. Again, I have no advice or useful information about moving. It just sucks and in the end there's a box of pens and knives. My house is going to look like boxes threw up everywhere forever. It's been two years in the new house now. There are still boxes. I have more pens and more knives. Who knows where that box went.

Remember those pancakes I made yesterday and put in the oven to keep warm? Yeah, I do too. Now.

Chapter 11

The Untimely Death of Mr. Sticker

You give up control. Then you realize you need control or the children will destroy the Christmas tree, and each other, and you must exert control or else the realtors won't sell your house and the whole world will end. It's an infuriating push-pull of parenting that I never know when to let go of the control and when to grab hold of the reins.

This push-pull came vividly into focus at my first son's one-year doctor's appointment when our doctor told us, "The most common cause of children's ER visits is household accidents."

My mind was abuzz. I just gave up on cleanliness and order. Wasn't that the answer? This lack of cleanliness, happiness solution said I should let go of control and order and be happy. No wait, I must control this. Quick, enact order! NO EMERGENCY ROOM VISITS! Buzzing, more thoughts came through.

I thought of calls we'd gotten when I worked in child welfare. Sometimes we got calls about kids who were really hurt in household accidents. I remembered some particularly dangerous ones that had happened, such as a kid who broke some bones falling out of a bucket car seat, when the parent tripped and fell while carrying the baby in it without buckling him in. No, this was not child abuse. I don't really remember why we got the call; I just remember the cautionary tale portion that stuck with me. I would never carry my infant around in the infant bucket seat unbuckled, the handle heavy in my hand. I could see why this could happen, but my family would never fall victim to this. CONTROL!

Still abuzz with the ER visit fears, I also thought of my friend's son. He had fallen off their half dozen front steps and been sent on a Flight-for-Life helicopter to a big children's hospital because he'd fractured his skull and his brain was swelling. He was four at the time. He had a shunt put in and is now fine, but it was terrifying for a bit. This particular kiddo had some stellar stories of things he'd done, including jumping (after the shunt) down a flight of stairs. Because "I can do anything, Mom" and what he determined he could do was fly. He could not be persuaded otherwise. He would hear of no argument from his mother against his impending capability of flying. This is the argument they had about it as recounted by his mother.

Mom "Right, but you can't fly. You don't have wings. Planes can fly. They have wings."

Kid: "What about super heroes? They don't have wings."

Mom, thinking quickly on her feet: "They have capes."

Kid: "Not Ironman. See, I can do anything if I try. I can fly."

So he "flew" down the entire stair case.

How does one control for such a child? He was sure to go to the ER, no matter what control his parents exerted.

I rushed home after the fear-instilling doctor's appointment. I thought of my own household and how it was inadequately childproofed. I must exert the control! We'd kept Mars alive a whole year. It was important to take the doctor's words to heart and continue the trend of keeping this baby alive. I began not only putting childproofing on the drawers and cabinets, but moving chemicals to higher up cabinets and putting things that couldn't hurt him like pots and pans in the lower cabinets of the kitchen. Towels under the sink in the bathroom replaced cleaning chemicals which went to a high up shelf in a hall closet. We had already anchored his dresser and bookshelf to the wall in his bedroom because I'd heard enough horror stories about how often children pull these things over on themselves to insist that this be done before he was even born. Pat, pat, Neurotic Me. "Good job, you controlled the book shelf!"

These new steps felt particularly good. I had discovered a new trick to keeping my tiny human alive and I was pleased. For about eight minutes.

The day after I did this, Mars did three things that convinced me that his safety was not within my control the way I'd wanted it to be.

I was making breakfast while Mars played on the kitchen floor. In fourteen seconds while I stirred the oatmeal, he managed to get the food processor out, click the pieces apart in the precise three-step order required to get the blade out, and lick it. I had run out of space in the higher up cabinets and hadn't thought he *could*, at twelve months of age, act as MacGyver to remove the blade. I was wrong. I gave birth to MacGyver, except the version of MacGyver who licks dangerous things.

The second thing was also while I was making breakfast. I had already taken away baby MacGyver's utility knife so he'd lost interest in the spoils of the kitchen. I finished setting out the food and looked around only to find he was missing. He had gone up our entire flight of stairs and into our bedroom. There, he climbed onto the bed, and by the time I got to him, he was climbing the headboard to reach a window above our bed designed to give a panoramic view of a mountain scape that was located five feet in the air, on the second floor of our house. I got him down and went to the trusty internet to purchase a baby gate for the stairs. So you'd think my day of childproof celebrations was back on track, but NO!

Because then while I was putting on my clothes after breakfast, he crawled into the bathroom. I confidently ignored him, knowing that he could only find towels in the cabinet under the sink, thanks to my genius ninja-mommy moves. So when I walked into the bathroom and noticed something was amiss with the way his jaw was set, I immediately asked,

"Mars, what's in your mouth?"

Because this was not the first time we'd had such a conversation, instead of replying, he simply opened his mouth. A fully-wrapped tampon plopped out of his mouth and down to the floor.

"THOSE HAVE TO BE UNDER THE SINK."

Yes, tampons are choking hazards. He did not choke; he was fine. The point being, childproofing only gets you so far.

When Gomez was just over a year, Rob had both boys out in the garage while he attempted to enforce some semblance of order to it, which sounds terrifying to me all on its own but not in the way it turned out to be. Rob had arranged several items in an arc so that the kids were basically trapped in the garage with him. He had his back turned, working, when he heard Mars say, "Look dad, Gomez's climbing the ladder, and he's doing really *good*!" Rob turned around to find Gomez ten feet in the air on our twelve-foot ladder. He got him down safely. But they really do these things *that* fast, even when you're right there. They just manage to do things.

It's a crapshoot. Sometimes you try your best and your kid falls off a few steps and has to have a shunt put in his skull. Other times (and I know two separate people who have had this happen) your toddler pushes against a screen window on the second floor which gives way and your child falls 15 feet to be totally fine (albeit under medical observation in a hospital for an excruciating and terror-filled 72 hours). Sometimes you childproof your home and your kid still gets ahold of a three-pronged blade and nearly chokes on a tampon. I really don't know how drug addicts raise children. The fact that any of us makes it to adulthood is truly a wonder of nature, or a miracle, or something.

I've exerted control where I could. I don't leave windows open where toddlers can push against screen windows. At least I try hard not to, but sometimes...I guess I'm saying I can see how easily it happens.

I did my best attempts at childproofing, going beyond those little plastic pieces that you attach to make it a pain for any adult to open any cabinet, and we anchored the dressers and bookshelves. Because I had a Baby MacGyver named Mars.

And now Mars is five. We've kept him alivc five years. And we've kept Gomez alive three years. So thanks to the times when control has worked and for the luck when it could have NOT worked. Because I really, really want to pick the right end of the push-pull relationship that is control in parenting so that my kids live a long, long time.

I had a dream I was stapling Mars to the inside of a box by his clothing to "wrap" him and send him to his grandmother for Christmas. We were both laughing so hard it was making it hard for me to properly use the staple gun. I might be nervous about Christmas.

Chapter 12

Flying Taco Ship

Sometimes I vividly imagine terrible accidents befalling my children. This started not long after I had my first baby. I'd picture someone falling down the stairs while holding him or the car reeling out of control with the baby in the car seat. Every other vehicle was the possible culprit of a fatal accident. I was exhaustedly vigilant. My imagination has since taken on a less fatal direction but the uncontrollable habit is still there.

I have a pretty active imagination and I can't always control where it goes. I also get anxious a lot, especially when I'm tired, which has been the last...uh...forever. So sometimes I picture terrible things befalling my children, sometimes I project their behavior into the future, and other times, I sit back and enjoy the weirdness that is parenting small children.

While writing this, my five-year-old is in a ski lesson and he's already fallen off the lift once to his death, and several times has fallen and broken an arm trying to learn to jump. But none of these things actually happened. I just imagined them, because I'm nervous. It's like my nervous mind moves too fast and needs something to do with the extra energy so I imagine the worst, sometimes in technicolor. I imagine Gomez falling down the stairs when he's carrying anything while going down the stairs. Like, even if he's just carrying a sock, I picture him falling down the stairs as I watch. I also imagine him falling down the stairs when he's got at towel wrapped around his shoulders. His body crashes and his arm is left at an odd angle. I also have a bizarre superstition that if I watch, this thing I'm imagining will actually happen and then I'll helplessly watch it happen in real time and it'll be my fault. Because I watched it happen and because I watched I made it happen. Yes, this is crazy.

As my kids have gotten past the baby stage, my imagination has turned on other of my children's behavior, not only perilous stuff they do like walk. Sometimes it's just whatever the kid happens to be doing, only I project that behavior into my kid's adulthood and am all like, "No, you can't lick ladies' toes! SHE SAID NO, YOU MANIAC!"

This is what happened in my head when Mars was a baby and decided to play with us the way we played with him. At the time, I would try to eat his toes. Yes, that sounds insane even as I type it now. And I swear I don't actually want to eat my children, but I do understand the especially strange cannibalistic outcries of parents and grandparents everywhere who just want to eat a baby up. It's completely counter to survival of the species to joke about eating each other. And, weirder still, I have totally put my kids' toes in my mouth and gummed them while making weird noises and laughing in bliss. Parenting is weird.

So smart little baby Mars initiated play with me by crawling over and biting my feet while I glided on the ottoman, and I'd project this behavior into the future and imagine that he was a creepster on the subway who attacked random women, only instead of pulling off a real attack, he just gummed her toes while saying, "I could just eat you up!" All this while living in our basement.

With Gomez, I didn't imagine him as an adult but an elementary student. Baby Gomez would, in a completely normal way, find lint on the floor and pick it up and put it in his mouth. Only I'd project him into elementary school where he'd be that weird kid in class that won't stop eating your papers and showing you the pulp before swallowing it. He also might lick some girl's eye. I'd get a call from the principal about this for sure.

One time on vacation while watching Sesame Street, Gomez was twirling around on the coffee table with Mars' underpants on. He had his entire body through one leg and was wearing them like a belt. I pictured him as a fabulous gay stripper. *Stop looking at my beautiful boy; he's not your man-meat, he's a person!*

It all depends on my level of anxiety whether I picture nothing at all, picture their behavior in the future, or picture horrible things happening.

Want to guess whether I pictured nothing and just laughed, pictured a horrible injury, or projected their behavior into adulthood?

Let's try it. I'll give you a real-life behavior I witnessed in one of my children, and you can guess whether I laughed, pictured something bad, or projected their behavior into adulthood. Here we go.

1. Gomez was on Mars' back in the bathtub yelling "yeah, horsey, neigh!!!" and giggling hysterically.
2. At three, Mars took all his clothes off and started saying "Naked Snake Shake" while sprinting and gyrating around the house.
3. When Mars was two he was at Gramma's with a couple of friends and no swim suits so they were getting in the hot tub naked. The oldest girl, 8, had a suit. Mars just kept saying "could you take that off? Pleeeease?" over and over again until, presto, she did!
4. At three Mars would run around naked yelling "NAKED PROBLEMS."
5. At Thanksgiving at our single friends' house, one of those apartments that bursts with singles in their twenties, when Mars was three, he asked this young gal if he could kiss her. She said yes and he laid one right on her lips. Then he asked if he could pour sugar all over her and eat it. He also kept trying to figure out ways to put his head on her cleavage, which was visibly substantial.

6. Mars brought me his grievance. Mars had gotten mad at Gomez and held out a pink piece of construction paper cut into an oval and folded in half: his evidence. He pointed at it and said "Gomez says it's a vagina but I don't like that because it's a flying taco ship."

Here they are again with answers:

1. Anxiety Level Medium-Gomez was on Mars' back in the bathtub yelling "yeah, horsey, neigh!!!" and giggling hysterically. I pictured a horrible adult future where the kids had an unhealthy attachment to one another. EW.
2. Anxiety Level Medium- At three, Mars took all his clothes off and started saying "Naked Snake Shake" while sprinting and gyrating around the house. I pictured Mars having a nudity problem in college and getting himself kicked out of the coed dorm.
3. Anxiety Level Low- Mars was at Gramma's with a couple of friends and no swim suits so they were getting in the hot tub naked. The oldest girl, 8, had a suit. Mars just kept saying "could you take that off? Pleeeease?" over and over again until, presto, she did! This could be a dangerous lesson, y'all. I picture Mars being WAY too successful with girls later and I really kind of suspect this to be true. Yes, this is technically projecting his behavior into the future, so if you're mad about whether you got it right or wrong because you're one of *those* people who keep score, well just give yourself the points. But my anxiety wasn't high. I just couldn't help but imagine that he'll be good with girls.
4. Anxiety Level High- Mars running around yelling "NAKED PROBLEMS." I have no idea why but it was just one of those moments when I pictured him falling and breaking a bone and me having to take him to the hospital and explain how he hurt

himself and how he was already naked because he just does that.

5. Anxiety Level Low- At Thanksgiving when Mars was three, and he asked this hot twenty-something gal if he could kiss her, then asked if he could pour sugar all over her and eat it. I don't know that I pictured anything because we were basically already at a frat house and oh my god, that boy!
6. Anxiety Level Low- Mars got mad at Gomez and held out a folded in half pink construction circle pointing at it and saying "Gomez says it's a vagina but I don't like that because it's a flying taco ship." And I promptly peed my pants because FLYING TACO SHIP!

(Pictured here. You'll notice, it happened to have the letter C on it).

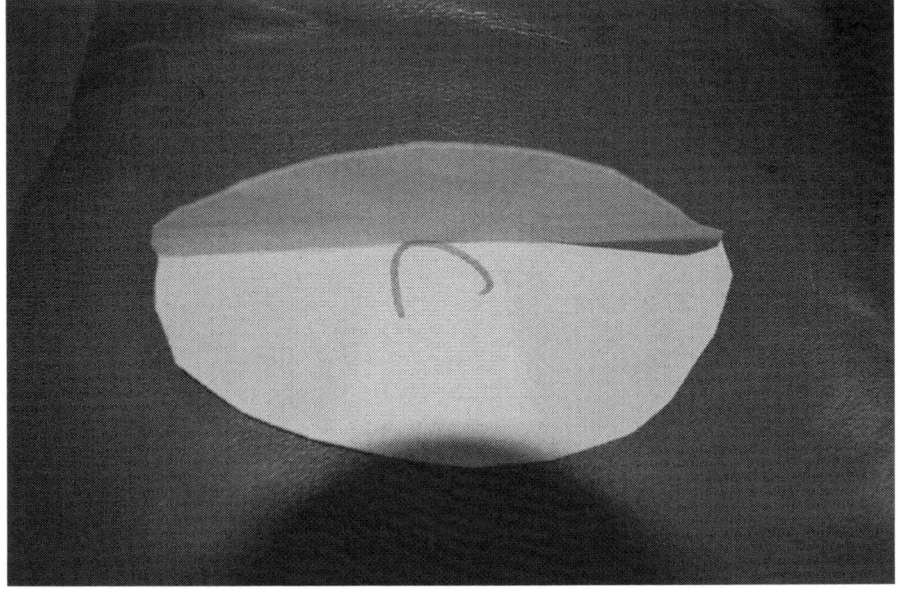

PART THREE
Toddlers are Really Detached Big Toes

Like taking bacon from a baby. But not like taking wood pellets or dog food. Those a baby would bite your fingers off for. Hopefully said baby has no teeth.

Chapter 13

Toddlers Eat Like Snakes

Introducing solid foods is an interesting shift that showcases the baby terrorist's first major chance at control and showing his opinions. I made Mars' baby food. A few of us moms got together. We all bought the same glass mason jars and then we'd each make two or so big batches of baby food and the jars with our baby food. We then brought our batches together for a swap. It seemed like the way to go at the time, despite the amount of effort it actually was because...uh...new moms are crazy people. And I was no exception. I made batch after batch and only fed Mars the homemade baby food that my crazy new-mom friends and I obsessively made.

Feeding Mars turned out to be way more fun to me than I'd have imagined. I've always been terrible about eating. I used to be one of those idiots who would forget to eat. Nothing says survival like "I forgot to eat."

I was surprised to find how much I enjoyed watching Mars try beets for the first time. I loved this time in our lives and seeing his reactions to new things. He loved beets and would do raspberries in a gleeful, albeit stain-inducing, expression of approval. He'd sit in his high chair which I'd put a towel underneath to handle the mess. I'd give him a spoonful of beets; his lips would turn bright and he'd say "bbbbssssppp!!!" He'd smile, clap, and sign "more" by taking his two fists and bashing them together and saying, "mo', mo'!"

I remember he would try any food. And sometimes even if he didn't like it, he'd try something over and over until it got silly. I have a video of him sucking on lemon slices, face scrunched up in protest, laughter, and then he'd shudder and repeat the whole process. He did it over and over. Lemon, screwed up face, shudder, giggle, bashing fists "mo', mo'!"

Then, when it was Gomez's turn, I bought a mini food processor, and planned to just grind whatever we were eating and feed it to him as baby food. This seemed more practical than the gourmet experience I'd provided for Mars, but still allowed me the bizarre obsession with making all the baby food.

Because Mars was a good eater, I mistakenly thought I'd done something right, that I could take credit for my child being a good eater. Oh no. Gomez had other ideas. Gomez started grabbing for <u>our</u> food at three months, but turned his nose up as soon as I finally gave in and tried giving him baby foods six weeks later. He definitely knew baby food was not what the rest of us were having, and he wanted no part of it. We ended up with two things that worked: give him tiny bites of whatever we were eating OR give him gigantic bites. These he couldn't choke on, and so he spent the dinner hour gumming them into a size he could deal with. He was entertained and happy at dinner then. In all reality, though, he wanted nothing to do with the foods we gave him as soon as he'd proven he could, in fact, pick them up himself and bring them to his mouth. At that point, he'd drop them on the floor like an MC drops the mic. "I did it, fools! Take that. Blech? Who eats this stuff?"

Except I think he signed all that. And by "signed" I mean he threw a mango pit on the ground and glared at us as though we'd intentionally insulted him by making his mouth taste like something other than milk. All this, despite his own obvious impressive effort and skill in picking up the item and tasting it. He simply didn't like food. He liked motor tasks.

Gomez has continued to be a pickier eater than Mars to this day. And all this boring stuff that you just stuck with reading (thank you for that), was essentially to demonstrate that 1. Kids are all different and what works with one kid won't necessarily work with another. And 2. Some kids are hard to get to eat.

Toddlers eat like snakes. They pick and turn their nose up at food for days. Then suddenly a new day dawns and they sit down and eat like pubescent linebackers at a medieval feast. "More cheeseburger, wench!" The best ways I've figured out for getting toddlers to eat are to wait until immediately after I've cleaned up a meal and am headed out the door. This is when they'll inevitably cry and whine about how they're starving. Alternatively, wait for bedtime. They're always hungry at bedtime.

I can't actually pull these strategies off because I'm too high strung and far more biologically driven to get calories into my children than I'd ever have predicted. I remember once nonchalantly, in an attempt to be supportive (before having children of my own), telling my friend that her kid would tell her if he was hungry or cold and so I was sure he was fine. What on earth did I know with my rationality and logic? I'm sure my "don't worry" strategy didn't do much for her then, so it might not do much for you either. It didn't work on me anyway.

Gomez, now 3, has been known to eat every last bite of food on his plate in a restaurant. But unpredictably and probably after about four days of eating barely anything. Because he eats like a snake. Most toddlers do.

Again, Mars and Gomez are different. Mars loved to eat as a toddler and even now still loves food. One time, we were so successful with getting Mars (then under 2) to eat, that he ate and ate and ate pork at lunch time. Eating pork for a young child seemed weird to me. I remember not liking meat as a kid because it was hard to chew. But if Mars could pick it up and eat it, he did. So that day, he ate an epic amount of pork right before nap. Then after nap, Rob came in and was all "What's in your mouth?" and it turned out Mars had a small piece of pork he was storing in his cheeks like a chipmunk, while sleeping, for two hours. He was a good eater AND a good food storer and never choked even when he tried to combine the two. But not so much with Gomez. With Gomez, he eats like a snake: large quantities every few days, unpredictably, and only when he wants to. And he's surviving and growing.

So if all else fails? Wait. Eventually they'll be pubescent linebackers and eat everything in sight, wench. Plus, in the meantime, they'll put all kinds of non-food items in their mouths. Sometimes they'll lick these items first before trying to eat them. Sometimes they just lick them and you'll never know why…

Gomez screeches in despair. Rob, holding up an empty ice cream container from the trash, tells him, "You can use this as a hat, but I'm going to rinse it out first."

Chapter 14

Stop Licking That!

When my oldest, Mars, was two, we went to a friend's for a bonfire some ways from town. It was a beautiful August afternoon. We wound our way up Ute Mountain Pass until the view nearly split the sky with sunshine and clouds colliding as we bumped our way up the gravel road. The view was of gray jagged ridgelines cut against blue skies with the occasional smear of nimbostratus clouds. We leveled off on a high plateau and in some places, you could see rain drops in the distance. They'd already been through and left a few puddles behind at our destination: a cabin in the mountains.

The approach to the cabin wound along the side of the house and ended about 100 feet from the doorway. Directly in front of the house stood a twenty-plus-year-old green, rusty, John Deere tractor. That is to say, it was picturesque.

There was so much open space you could feel your breath release. We parked and found our friends around a fire pit where a goat was almost finished roasting on a spit. It sizzled and popped and the gravel crunched under our dusty feet. After we'd parked, I relaxed and let Mars run off and try to keep up with the other kids who were a bit older. Rob and I took turns looking out for Mars and when I saw Rob return from the cabin, looking worn out from the chase, I stood from my log at the fire to trade off and take my turn supervising kids.

The kids were chasing each other in a circle around the tractor. I approached, joining in, chasing one and then another kid. I stopped when I realized Mars had climbed the tractor. I was heading around to make sure he didn't fall, only to find, he was now licking standing water off its rusty hood.

"Stop licking that!"

I had to tell my kid to stop licking standing water off a rusty tractor. And this was when there was a parent child ratio of two to one. Now there are two of them and two of us. I will tell you the amount of licking and ingesting non-food items has not improved. Gomez is even worse about these things than Mars was. At three, Gomez thinks it's hysterical to lick things and is not to be persuaded otherwise. If you attempt it, he will laugh with abandon and deny any consequence with persistence. He loves to lick things. Loves.

Top 10 things I have told my children not to lick other than standing water off a rusty tractor:

1. The vinyl booth at a family restaurant
2. The table top at the same restaurant approximately fifteen seconds after the booth
3. The handle of the grocery cart at least a dozen times
4. The dusty side of our Highlander during a snowy mountain winter...mmm...salty
5. My FACE
6. Each other's faces
7. The dog whose nickname is Pierre Pooppaw. Gross, right?
8. Grosser still, each other's butts
9. A puddle in the street
10. And the winner? A public bathroom stall door. Horrible, horrible...horrible.

Honorable mention goes to Gomez for licking chapstick off of a playdough cookie he made himself. Or "icing," as he called it.

Recently, my coworker mentioned that while my five-year-old was in my office one day and I was talking with a colleague in the hall, she peeked into my office and saw him licking the second drawer of my filing cabinet. She winked and smiled at him and he laughed and kept going. She has three boys. THREE.

One morning, when Gomez was not quite two, he lay down in the cul-de-sac in front of gramma's house and lapped up water from a gravel-filled puddle like a dog. I trudged over, picked him up and the whole front side of his body—hands, face, chest—was covered in black water. That time, I didn't even bother to tell him not to lick the puddle.

When I told a girlfriend of mine the title of this book, she told this story. She had recently been out of town with her two girls who are 3 and 6 years old. She said her dad pulled her aside to tell her how lovely it was to watch her care for everyone. "But," he told her, "You're so busy caring for everyone else, that I saw something you missed the other day. Your daughter was licking her sister's armpit." So while this book is about raising boys, it could just as easily have been about raising girls, apparently. Because that girl licked her sister's armpit.

I started off joking that I'd write a funny book about the ridiculousness that is raising these two boys who lick things. I took the cover photo and kept a list (that grows to this day) of all the things they've licked. But the more I worked on the book, the more I realized how much this is really what the book is about. Parenting is as simple and as hard as getting your kids to stop licking things. You tell them not to. They laugh and do it anyway. Parenting is bizarre and you find yourself doing and saying things you never thought you'd ever, ever say like "stop licking your brother's butt" and "don't worry, you won't pull your penis off" and "it's a present? Really, for me? Thanks, buddy, I'd love to take that bite you already chewed up." You imagine your life one way. They laugh in the face of reason, and you do it all differently.

At three, Gomez shot a fruit snack out of his nose, snot rocket-style and then immediately yelled "It's not yucky!" and started crying because I threw it away and he'd still wanted to eat it.

Chapter 15

Stockholm Syndrome

Getting pregnant changes you some, and getting used to a new baby is another thing that changes you some, but then what will truly teach you what you're made of is having a real, live, wholly himself toddler. You get through the exhaustion and bizarre side effects of pregnancy and infants, and give up a bunch of control, and then you really have to find out what you're made of.

If there was any remaining lie I told myself about what an awesome parent I would be, having a threenager dissolved it. I am who I am, and I struggle to parent. I struggle to parent because it's hard, because I care about trying to do it right, and yet I am still a woefully willful woman, trying to parent irrational toddler terrorists with their own ideas and opinions. Ideas and opinions which change constantly. And trying to appease said terrorists, makes you feel a bit like uh...you have Stockholm syndrome. Here's an example of me and my Stockholm syndrome.

It started at night.

Gomez got up and came to my bed.

"I had a dream about a robot." He melted into me and I scooped him up and whisked him to the extra bedroom, where I mostly didn't sleep the rest of the night. Gomez slept but I just enjoyed the snuggles and dozed. I was bonding with my captor. I finally drifted off in the wee hours and awoke in full sun. The light alerted me to how late we'd slept. By then, I had to pee really bad and so I started to get up.

"Wait for me, Mommy," Gomez whined.

I hesitated for a moment, but I really had to go, so I went without him. And then this happened for twenty minutes.

"I WANTED TO WATCH YOU PEE, MOMMY. MOMMY, I WANTED TO WATCH YOU PEE," he screamed, while crying and writhing on the floor.

In a short moment, my mind was taken over by my toddler. His terrorist mentality caused me to fear for my life. Would he be more upset if I flushed or didn't flush? Maybe I could tell him that I hadn't flushed and he could pee on my pee. This is a bizarrely effective tactic I have used a lot in the latter stages of potty training. It's for when the toddler is too busy and so doesn't want to go to the potty, but it really *is* time. So I tell him, "You can go peepee on my peepee." I know – bizarre. But it works. I give him a two option choice - he can pee on my pee, or I can pee on his pee. This has worked on both my kids to get them to go the bathroom when it's time to leave or they're ornery in the morning and they're about to pick an irrational power struggle about the bathroom. Worst power struggle ever. You can't win. They can't win. It's a struggle and no one wins. In fact, you both lose when they have an accident, making you all really late to wherever you were heading.

Back to the instance at hand. Gomez was screaming about the fact that I peed and I was deciding if I could use the pee-on-my-pee tactic except, I couldn't remember if I'd flushed. And I wanted to have *not* flushed because then I could maybe negotiate with my terrorist captor for a ceasefire. But then I also worried that if I'd flushed already, Gomez would be triggered into an emotional bombing. He might go limp and scream "I WANTED TO DO THAT!"

He might cry that he wanted to pee on my pee. Or he might not.

And this is Stockholm syndrome. You know the thing where a victim becomes attached to her captor even though he's a terrorist? Only I'm an adult mom and my terrorist captor is less than 3 feet tall. I worry that leaving my urine, which I very much needed to have exit my body in its own time, might be an insult to the terrorist, and a reminder of how I didn't wait and let my toddler watch. Me. Pee.

Or if I did flush, he might be equally mad that he could not pee on my pee, AND that I had not allowed *him* to flush.

I had a few reactions. I laughed. I ignored him and lay in the bed for as long as possible with pee in the toilet that I may or may not have been able to use as a negotiation tactic. I was tired. I considered whether I might survive by simply keeping the covers over my head and never leaving the bed. But not feeding him soon would only make it worse. And I thought, "Man, this is weird. Also, crazy."

Toddlers are terrifying creatures. Especially at three. And if you can avoid a meltdown, no matter how crazy it sounds to do something, you'll do it. You'll let them go first or second to pee. You'll let them use your hand to flush the toilet. You'll negotiate with terrorists.

The old adage about terrible twos is complete nonsense. Most two-year-olds are easy. They're into making choices, they like climbing and the swings. They're easy to trick. They love their mommies.

As they get older though, it's harder and harder. They push your buttons. Heck, they install new buttons in you just so they can push them. The worst age is three.

The key to surviving a threenager is patience. And if you don't have it, join the stinky, exhausted, messy house-havin' club.

If you have inadvertently flushed a toilet after insulting your captor, just blow the whole toilet up. Because you cannot win. You can only attempt to negotiate. And you'll lose.

When Mars was four, he and Rob raced me and Gomez to the bottom of the sledding hill. Mars came up to me at the finish and said, "Tooters don't get trophies."

Chapter 16

Detached Big Toes

Mars' threenager stage started around 16 months and lasted almost four years. This is not typical but what did I know? At sixteen months, Mars would laugh this non-funny laugh at any punishment. At two, and three, and even at four, he would throw things at the door, and scream if put in time out. I vividly remember a fit he threw at two.

"Mars, we're going to check out the chocolate train at Keystone. You *have* to put on your snowsuit so we can go."

"Nnnnnooooooo," he whined and flailed on the carpet.

He'd awoken from nap and my cousin was in town. We were all supposed to meet up at the resort to go look at this huge and elaborate chocolate display which gets new additions each year. It's an annual tradition to travel the ten minutes to look at the display, remark on what's new in it, then have hot chocolate with gourmet chocolate from Rocky Mountain Chocolate Factory.

"Mars, don't you want to go eat chocolate with your cousins?" His cousins are his favorite people ever. They are up there with gods in his personal hierarchy of humans.

"Eh…" he whined, arching his neck and stiffening his body.

We went back and forth some more with our negotiations. I figured he'd just woken up and I wanted to give him a chance to fully wake up and realize that obviously going to look at, and *eat* chocolate, was awesome and he wanted to do that, but he was having no part of it.

"Mars, don't you want to have chocolate? Everyone's going. I can help you put your snowsuit on," I offered.

"NO!"

I waited. "We're running out of time, buddy. How about I help you put on your snowsuit?"

I laid it on the floor and tried putting him on top of it. He recoiled, screamed, and rolled away.

"Mars, if you don't get ready soon, you can't come. You can't come have chocolate with us and see the chocolate train." I enunciated chocolate as clearly as I could.

What two-year-old boy doesn't want to see a fully locomotive train made of chocolate?

"NOOO!!!"

"Okay, Anna and I are going to go without you and you'll stay here with Daddy if you don't let me help you put your snowsuit on."

"Nnnnnooooooo." More whining and flailing ensued. I tried putting him in the suit again but he arched his back and flopped around and I gave up.

We went without him. Epic to-the-finish fits are just what he did.

For Mars this stage was all-consuming and lasted years and ultimately required some professional help to teach him the calming part. More on that later.

Meanwhile, for Gomez, at least so far, this stage has been short and sporadic. The case where he was a terrorist captor, needing to pee, was an isolated incident. He rarely throws a fit that lasts. It's happened, sure, but with manageable infrequency. Usually, his fits are brief and if you either figure out what went wrong or put him in timeout, he resets with a snuggle and is perfectly fine again. But he does have his moments.

The thing about three that makes them threenagers is their development. There's this whole idea of themselves as separate beings they're trying to come to terms with. Before about three years old, babies essentially think they are the same person as their primary caregivers. It's a survival thing. They bond to the adult who can do amazing tasks, like figure out where his hand is in space and use that hand to do things like survive.

"Woah, magical creature, you understand how to use those hands? You must be the leader part of my body! Help, magical leader."

Babies bond so strongly, that they think of themselves as the same as the caregiver. They go, hey, we're hungry. Cry-cry, why haven't you noticed we're hungry? Cry some more, and then the caregiver feeds them something. Since the caregiver could obviously sense how uncomfortable being hungry felt, and solve the problem, that reinforces the idea the caregiver and the baby are the same. That crazy bond is the healthy basis of communication. Baby cries, caregiver correctly interprets cry and baby has communicated! And also bonded. This is the basis for all the other important higher functions the baby develops later. Weird, yes, but also helpful. Bond closely with caregiver, get needs met, deal with inaccuracies later. It's a bit like politics, actually. Hmmm...

Then around three, the kid's all like, wait a second! I'm hungry and you haven't noticed. I cried and you said "give me a minute." You and I are DIFFERENT! You are not hungry and ***I*** am. We're not the same! And it makes them a little crazy and that's good, because the toddler and the adult are not actually the same person and probably the toddler needs to learn that. Also, we all have things that get us a little crazy and we have to learn calming strategies to deal with those things.

You, me, separate. And that's what three-year-olds are doing. They're learning they're separate from you, this hurts, this makes them crazy, and they have to learn how to deal.

It would be like if suddenly you found out your big toes could hop off your feet and do their own thing. Sure, a toe could do some things on its own, but it'd really still need the rest of you to go very far. And frankly, you need your big toe to get back on board to walk anywhere and do anything.

Just like big toes, if a toddler tries to get too far without you, you're going to trip and fall all over the sidewalk.

Such is the life of a three-year old. *I CAN DO IT MYSELF, MOMMY!* And what they're trying to do themselves is to rip their hand away from you to walk through the parking lot alone. They're too short for that nonsense.

"Cars can't see you, baby."

"Carry me!"

Detached toe throws himself on the concrete.

They need you, and they're mad at you when it doesn't work, or isn't the idea they had. And you're in a parking lot holding more bags than any one person should be capable of holding. Meanwhile, they're standing somewhere refusing to move unless you carry them. And that somewhere is the middle of the road. You then attempt to carry all the bags and the kiddo. You achieve getting to your car, sweating and dropping bags, but you make it.

While giving up on some apples rolling through the parking lot, you think, "I'll get those in a minute."

You've almost got this. Almost. But then you make a mistake in the car entrance.

"No, Mommy, *I* buckle mahself!"

He likes to buckle himself. But only the top buckle. And only after you lined it up. But in your hurry to recover your torn groceries which are spreading through the parking lot, you buckled it for him.

"YOU BUCKLED IT? I WANTED TO DO IT MAHSELF!" You now have a screaming, hysterical mess on your hands. And the only solution is to take him out, set him down in the parking lot, and restart the entire routine again from the beginning or else it will not end. But if you get the combination right, the terrorist will let you live.

You accomplish buckling and exhale after buckling yourself. You do not start the car. You pant.

Thus steeled for whatever the afternoon may bring, you start the car and hand him a graham cracker, thinking this will get you home.

"But Mommy, I wanted it in one BIG piece, and now it's broken!"

There are endless examples of how your child finds out you and he are not the same person. And the indignation? Oh, it's fierce. "How DARE you break my graham cracker into pieces, you barbarian!" That's what your toddler's eyes are saying, if you're wondering.

How could you not know I want to sit on the *blue* chair at the restaurant? This, despite the fact that the blue chair is mounted to the wall and sized for a mouse. Mommy can solve everything and she should know what I'm thinking as a toddler because we're the same. Until she doesn't know what he knows, and doesn't do what he wants, and then he melts at the realization that he and mommy are NOT the same! And then said toddler tries to assert himself similarly to a big toe.

Utter meltdown. And you're on the sidewalk unable to do anything until you figure out how what to do with a detached big toe terrorist.

With some things you can wait it out, and let them make the choices and do the strange things they want to do. You can start over with the seat belt. Sometimes honoring their autonomy works. You can take them back out, and let them start over. Set him on the side walk. Let him climb back into the car. Help him position himself. Let him buckle the top of the seatbelt. You then ask as politely as possible if you can buckle the bottom. He lets you. SUCCESS!

If you've ever interrupted a toddler who has just learned to dress himself by "helping" with his shirt, only to have him rip it off in hysterics, and take off all the rest of his clothes too so he can do it himself, then you know what I'm talking about. At this stage, they need to have their autonomy respected and honored by letting them put their own clothes on in their specific order.

And you may need to scream into a pillow. Or rip up papers. Or as I did one time when my kids could *not* stop arguing while painting, smear a brushstroke or six of water-based paint over their faces. Seriously, that was a pretty awesome way to take out my frustration. Yes, I literally reached over and painted smears right down their little faces and I will tell you it felt great. They laughed like gigglepusses and then painted their own faces and were utter messes. They stopped bickering. I felt better. Then they got a bath. Everyone won!

You have to figure out what weird things you can do to release the tension and you have to figure out what weird things you can let them do. The image on the cover is a perfect example of this. Let them wear a winter hat and sunglasses to the bathroom in May. Honor their autonomy and let them make choices that don't matter to you when you can.

You can also put all the unpredictable awesome things they do while being their own creative selves into your mind. When Gomez was eighteen months old (before threenagerness,) his favorite thing to do was be naked with one Croc on, and climb into the bathroom sink while sucking on any toothbrush he could get his hands on. This was admittedly weird and I did take pictures. I'll not include them here, as I'd like him to be speaking to me when he's in high school, at least until I show the pictures to his prom date.

When you're getting furious at the detached big toe of a toddler throwing a fit with all the usefulness of a bloody toe, it's helpful to remember the awesome things that they do and do your best to remain calm. I'm not awesome at the calm part but I am awesome at remembering cool things they've done. For example, I remember walking in on Gomez kissing Batman's helicopter. Remembering that he kissed Batman's helicopter helps me unbuckle his car seat and let him try even though I'm aggravated and I'd like to get on with it, already.

I remember Gomez putting a metal colander on his head, banging it with a spoon, and calling himself "baker man." I think of this when he wants to push a specific pattern of buttons on the blender and I let him.

I remember once getting an afternoon alone with Gomez when he was two. Alone time with your second is a rare and precious gift not to be squandered on a mere trip to the grocery store or paltry housework. Instead, we ran from imaginary sheep monsters and hid behind the bedroom door in the hall closet. We giggled and took fifteen minutes vacuuming a four-foot square of carpet.

It has helped both kids threenagerness when I spend individual, focused time with them and let them choose what we do. You have to find a way to draw attention to what you're doing though. When I'm really on top of my parenting game, I set a timer and let the threenager choose what we do for a few minutes and call it Mommy-and-me Time. I did this with Mars while Gomez napped. Or at a time when he was turning into kind of a jerk and I could tell he really could benefit from one-on-one time and attention. I'd tell Mars, "As soon as Gomez is asleep, we'll do Mommy-and-Me Time." He knew this meant that he got my full focus and he'd get to decide what we did. Sometimes this bought me enough time to get Gomez down for a nap.

It's hard to remember to do though, because down time is so valuable. And usually I'm eager to use that downtime to get the one kid occupied so I can accomplish a tad of the TON of stuff I haven't gotten to, like brush my teeth. Still, setting a timer for five minutes and letting the threenager, detached toe, terrorist lead us to doing what he wanted for five minutes made a far bigger impact on our relationship than all the discipline I'd done before the timer. His compliance improved better because of the time we spent together than it would have with ten timeouts and overall the few timed minutes together adds up to far less time than all the time it takes to discipline. Mars still asks for Mommy-and-Me Time, and it's been years since we started doing that. It's really powerful and effective.

You have to put deposits into the memory bank of awesome moments. It's hard to stay mad when you picture your kid naked with one croc and a stolen toothbrush and a giant grin on his face. Things like your kid kissing Batman and Mommy and Me Time and watching him be a baker man with a metal colander on top of his head are great to add to the memory bank. Thinking of these helped me to survive the moments where they acted like a detached big toe, bleeding all over my white pants. Because they had those moments. Also, therapy. Therapy is so, so good.

Saturday Gomez got a sunburn on his lips. This morning all Gomez wanted was frozen blueberries. This meant that despite cleaning off his face, I sent him to daycare looking like he'd been drinking red wine all night.

Chapter 17

Toddlers are Unpredictable

Threenagers are not always terrorists. Sure they have those moments, but they're also hilarious little humans. The awesome side of them finding out they're a different person than their caregivers is that they become their own person and you can't predict how this'll play out. You give up the necessary amount of control, and sit back to find out exactly who the toddler you're raising is becoming. It is both unpredictable and entertaining, like if you were watching the blossoming of a rubber chicken. Toddlers do hilarious things. Here are three of my favorite unpredictable and funny things my kids have done.

Dragon Rider

One morning, the boys were playing together. Mars was on all fours on the hallway floor, and Gomez was riding on his back. Mars had a stud-finder that he was holding to his throat and white guitar picks in his mouth. Gomez had a car attached to one foot that he was rolling along the floor beside them. They were still in their jammies and pretending to be characters in a dragon show who has white teeth (guitar picks) and shoots an electric shock (stud-finder noise). The dragon also has a rider with no left foot, which is why Gomez had the car on his foot.

The Splash Pad

One night while I was teaching at our local community college and my husband was (heaven forbid) going to the bathroom, he heard the front door open and close. The boys, then 2 and 4, had been playing in the living room prior to the door slam. My husband finished up quickly and headed out the door to investigate. He reached the deck, which overlooks our unpaved driveway to find our boys. Naked. It turned out that when he thought they were playing nicely, they were really taking off all their clothes. By the time he found them, they were jumping in a pot hole filled with wet gravelly rainwater at the end of the driveway, naked. Did I mention they were naked? Because they were naked.

"What are you doing?" he asked.

Mars answered incredulously, "We're playing in the splash pad at the end of the driveway!" I picture that this was in that duh-uh tone that kids are ever-so-good at. "That's how they do it in the city, Dad! They dig a hole and fill it with water."

Naked.

Hobos on Nine Year's Eve

When my son Mars was three, we went to a New Year's party at a friend's. We celebrated Nine Year's Eve, which is what happens when you get old and lame and have kids, but still want to have a cocktail with your friends. So you let the kids stay up until a whopping 9:00 p.m. and then, since they can't tell time, tell the kids it's New Year's.

Gomez was a baby at the time and slept through the entire affair. Meanwhile, at 9:00 p.m. the toddlers went rabble-rousing through the neighborhood with their pots and pans a'bangin'. They returned and huddled on the stairway landing with a bottle of non-alcoholic sparkling cider that had so much sugar in it we could have just given them a bowl of sugar and three spoons. Since the adults were busy talking and the kids weren't complaining, we let them have at it and sure enough, the vagrants drank the entire bottle. The only way I'd have pictured them more as hobos is if they'd actually had their bottle in a brown paper bag. In all reality, they used cups. Or well, they started with cups, and finished with the bottle. In a brown paper bag. Don't worry, they only start shooting up on the corner if you let them stay up until midnight. Or something.

By 10:00 p.m., we shuffled into our house, set the already-sleeping kids in their beds and went to bed ourselves. It was awesome.

Surprised that Mars was still asleep at seven the next morning, unusual for him, I padded down the stairs to make coffee and breakfast by myself. Typically, I made breakfast with Gomez in a carrier on my back in between Mars grabbing my legs and whining for something, but on this sunny morning, I would get to make coffee and breakfast in glorious solitude. I must've spun on my heel in my Donna Reed dress with my makeup just so. Yeah right.

Upon arriving downstairs, I found a large pile of candy wrappers spread in a three-foot circle on the floor.

I was confused. These had definitely not been there the night before.

I continued to the kitchen where I found two mugs on the counter filled with water. They each contained a balled-up wad of mixed colored playdough in the bottom.

What on earth?

I left the kitchen and went to the family room. There I found another circle of candy wrappers. None of this had been there the night before. So, instead of making coffee, a vital first step in starting my morning, I went back up the stairs. At the top of the stairs, I realized that the door to our extra bedroom was open; I'd missed this detail when I first got up. The light in the room was on, and there was Mars, face-down and perpendicular to the bed, asleep. This was not where he'd been laid down to sleep the night before.

Clearly when Mars awoke after his sugar high wore off, he'd wanted to keep partying, an idea which further supports my now-sepia image of the three-year-olds huddled with their paper bags and sugar spoons full of smack.

Mars had awoken sometime in the night and instead of finding me, he'd gotten up and had himself a one-man party. I pictured him, footy pajamas muffling the sound of him sneaking down the carpeted stairs to the living room, where he located his felt Christmas stocking full of goodies. He ate as much candy as his tiny fingers were agile enough to open. Then with his latest fix of smack in his system, he moved on. He located playdough, already hardened from being left out unsealed. He had been dissatisfied with the dry playdough, so he sought to remedy the situation. He pulled the step stool to the sink. Using the step stool, he climbed onto the counter, opened the cupboard, and got out a coffee mug. He climbed back down with the mug and filled it with water, then plopped the play dough in to steep. Then he did it again for the second ball of dried-up playdough.

His task finally complete, he went back to get his next fix and found more candy. He again ate the items he could open. Then he ran in crazy toddler circles until he plum wore himself out. Maybe he checked on his playdough to see that it had still not returned to the pliable softness that leaves its smell on your hands (blech), so he gave up, his blood sugar dropped, and he dragged himself back up the stairs. Heck, maybe it hadn't completely dropped yet. Maybe he was still a'partying and flipped the switch on in the extra bedroom, and jumped on the bed until he fell and bonked his head and passed out cold. I actually have no idea. I don't know how long he was up or what all he did. All I know for sure is that he left piles of candy wrappers on the floor and playdough soaking in coffee cups of water and that he was asleep in a different bed in the morning than where he started the night before, with the light on and face-down perpendicular to the bed. He clearly had himself a time.

I wasn't there. I was asleep and thought he was too! He slept until 10:00 a.m. without ever waking anyone, he has still (at nearly 6) never slept so late since that day.

This is by far my favorite Mars story because unlike with other parenting stories where whatever normal parent I talk to has a similar or related story, this one is always met with shock. No one else seems to have a story like this about such a young child. And that's Mars.

A discussion with Mars about men.

"How do you know when someone is a man?"

"I don't know."

"Is the exchange student across the street a man?"

"No! He's a student. And students can't be mans. They're teenagers."

Chapter 18

Toddler or Unruly Friend?

Now that you've learned all about my toddlers, let's play Toddler or Unruly Friend - the game where you guess whether the quote or behavior was performed by an unruly friend or a toddler. Ready? Here we go.

1. "I'm not going to tell you about the syrup. I drank it for a snack."
2. Two naked people are found "showering" in the curtain sheers.
3. The delivery man got talked into wearing a tuck 'n tale.
4. That blue water really cleans my hands, but it sure tastes terrible.
5. "You may not EVER pee in a cooler at my house again."
6. "Keep it in your pants, buddy."
7. "But, I'm pretending to pee red."
8. "I super-glued Spiderman's butt back on. I'm pretty much ready to conquer the world."
9. Ben wanted to 'help' so he scrubbed the toilet with mascara and then painted his face with it.
10. Waiting in the principal's office in a kiddie chair, makes me want to write the F word on the wall in smelly marker.
11. "This is how Chinese ladies fight dragons" while holding a drink umbrella overhead and making jabby motions with a drink sword.
12. Naked jumping on a bed doing the chicken dance only the clapping part is done on naked buttocks.

13. Peeing on a fire hydrant is as gross as you think it is. It does spray the exact way you imagine. Very. Bad. Idea.

Answers: (1. toddler, 2. toddler- together they're worse than two unruly friends, 3. adult 4. toddler, 5. toddler, 6. toddler, 7. adult, 8. toddler, 9. adult, 10. toddler, 11. toddler, 12. adult)

PART FOUR
Parenting Involves So Much Gross And Weird Stuff

I totally wiped one of Gomez's boogers on our boxer dog. After all the times Pierre Poop-paw has slimed us, I figure he had it coming.

Chapter 19

Sprinted ShitPrints

Having kids all around encouraged me to up my gross-ness quotient and I love it. Mostly. I remember Mars complaining about stubble in my armpits and making a face about it one morning. My reaction was to smoosh his face right in there and laugh maniacally. This is what is spectacular about where I'm at in life right now. I laugh openly about it all. And it's a good thing.

There are also moments where it is helpful if you can save the sense of humor for afterward and use your poker face in the moment. Because parenting involves poop and more. Even grosser things than poop, but let's start with poop.

From the moment of conception to some theoretical time I haven't happened upon yet, parenting means poop. Jokes about poop. Actual poop. Toys that, on the ground and without proper vision correction, look like poop. Which toys, you ask?

- A rubber Chewbacca figurine

- Mr. Potato Head's mustache

- All brown Duplo Legos
- Cat barf—and yes, yes it is messed up to be relieved that it *is* in fact cat puke because it means it is *not* kid poop. And this is nothing compared to seeing something brown smeared on your forearm and being scared because of the worst guessing game in parenting: "Poop or Chocolate?" No one wins.

I thought changing diapers was going to be the annoying part of parenting and then I had a baby and didn't really care that much about the diaper changes. But then stamina became a real killer because I didn't mind individual diaper changes, but the accumulation of four years of changing diapers every day did wear on me, especially multibutt, back-to-back diaper changing. BUT, the diapers are the least of it. It's more the overall emphasis on poop. It's constant and yet varied. Here are some examples.

 I'd enter Mars in a contest for the most times pooping in a hole. Every hike, every camping trip.

 Gomez has definitely got the record for the most times pooping in an airplane bathroom. I count three on a two-day trip to California. The only other time he pooped on the trip was in a sand hole on the beach. So he must've heard about Mars and his pooping in a hole championship. He's making a go at the record.

 When Gomez was two, he took his diaper off one morning and dropped it down one leg of his jammies, then he pooped down the other leg. Due to footie pajamas, the problem was contained (sort of).

But the winner of all poop stories for me is this:

One evening when Mars was 14 months old, I went to change his diaper after dinner. I took the diaper off and cleaned him up in our downstairs before I realized I didn't have diapers down there. I'd had wipes but no diapers. So I went upstairs to get a diaper. Mars was so thrilled with his naked bottom that he started sprinting back and forth across the living room floor at full speed. Rob was sitting right there so I literally ran up the stairs and then right back down.

"What the— seriously, Rob?" I exclaimed when I arrived back downstairs.

"Huh?" he said, looking up from a book.

Mars was still sprinting. Back and forth and back and forth as fast as he could with poop up his leg. Plus there were brown footprints all across the white carpet.

"Mars just pooped everywhere!"

He'd pooped *while* sprinting. He'd sprinted shitprints all across the floor and his own feet.

(Note: never begin a diaper change without *all* necessary supplies.)

(More important note: parenting involves so, so much weird and gross stuff.)

Once when Gomez was two, he took a dump at Noodles & Co that was longer than the song, American Pie. Seriously.

Chapter 20

Don't Push Potty Training

When Gomez was born, Mars was only two. Gobs of people have their kids two years apart and I'm constantly shocked by that because of exactly how hard that was. A two-year-old is not self-sufficient. I was terrified to have a second kid because my first kid was still literally sprinting away from me every time I set him down. I'd get him out of the car seat, set him down in the driveway and he'd be sprinting toward the busy street, so much so that I stopped setting him down until I could put him inside the house. I put the kid on a sticker chart to convince him to walk up the stairs himself, because at two, they don't always do that themselves either.

"Carry me upstairs, but I'll sprint down the driveway toward traffic!" Good Lord.

For me, the adjustment to having one kid was fine. I know that's not the case for everyone, but I'd been around my niece a lot when she was first born, and I'd seen my friends raising kids up-close, so I had a pretty realistic idea of how much you change diapers and don't sleep and how you rearrange your schedule to accommodate naps and bedtimes and basically redo your whole life. I had been ready to have Mars. I had wanted the changes.

But adjusting to having two children was much harder for me, and having two in cloth diapers was really intense. I was washing diapers every other day and trying to figure out how to have them both survive and not eat things that are not edible or get hold of knives, and that was harder than I imagined. Mars wasn't potty trained. He couldn't dress himself. He couldn't simply be laid down for a nap. He still woke up in the middle of the night. He couldn't be trusted not to draw all over everything if he found a pen or even be trusted *not* to put things in the toilet if he had access to things or the toilet. And, if you're going to teach them to use the toilet, you have to give them access to the toilet and give them things.

And Mars put things in the toilet. Things like the remote control. I remember one Christmas going to the store to buy a new remote only the store was out and so we just gave up and stopped watching anything for a while because we'd already replaced the remote three times before that time and dang, if they're out of universal remotes and this is your fifth one, mayhap it's time to just give up for a while, hmm?

To prepare for baby two, we got Mars out of the crib and into a big boy bed. We got rid of his pacifier months before his brother came along so that he wouldn't resent the baby or constantly steal his pacifiers. I assembled a special kit of toys for Mars to use during feedings and putting the baby down for naps. I read books to Mars about being a big brother and talked with him about the baby in my tummy often. We put temporary tattoos on our bellies and talked about the baby.

All that prep and, moments after the birth of Gomez, Mars stepped into the room. He looked at the bundled up new baby, smiled, then frowned with concern for this tiny new person. "But who are his mom and dad?"

Oh you poor, poor soul. *We're taking them away from your singular attentions and you'll have to share yours…*Obviously this is not what we said. I think we just laughed our butts off and waited for him to figure it out himself.

The parenting books will tell you not to push potty training until the child shows readiness signs. I think the signs are when the kid can actually write the words "I want to poop in the big potty" on a sign, walk out to the highway, and hold it until he has collected enough spare change to put down a house payment. I actually don't know because I was beginning to lose my patience with Mars' giant craps and so I didn't wait to see all the signs happen. Instead, (*whole audience gasps*) I pushed him.

Resenting diaper changes is no good, but let me tell you, pushing a kid to potty train isn't awesome either. Especially a kid who is having some trouble adjusting to a new brother. And if you're like me, you might totally ignore this advice because you're getting angry about the amount of time you're spending washing your hands before and after the fifty diaper changes a day. All while the older kid is explaining what he wants you to do when you're done changing his diaper. But before you're done changing the diaper, he's busy complaining about how you're supposed to use this cream, not that, and telling you which pants to put back on him. It was irritating to have a child so verbal and directive who took adult-sized poops in diapers.

Choose the evil you can live with. And now I will illustrate why the parenting books are right: you should not push potty training before they're ready.

I was ready. *I* pushed potty training. We got the potty and the Elmo video and I don't remember what all else we did. Taking clothes off yourself is supposed to be a readiness sign. And Mars learned to take his own clothes off. I know because I remember turning around in the kitchen at my brother's birthday party that May, all the guys holding shots aloft, bolstering themselves with birthday wishes in preparation for the shots, and Mars (just over two and a half then) waltzed in naked. "Oh hi, guys!" he said, and a roomful of men erupted in deep, uproarious laughter. He marched through nonplussed. Surely he was ready. But the thing is, he hadn't taken said clothes off, taken a shot of whiskey with the men, and posted a sign about it on an overpass. He wasn't ready, see? Because he couldn't quite spell yet.

Elmo video at the ready, I pushed, and for a while it seemed to be working. Mars took his own clothes off and sometimes went in the potty. YAY!

He was doing great with the potty until Gomez became interactive. With Gomez sitting up and taking up more of mom's time and energy, Mars had to think of something and fast. It's common for kids with new siblings to regress in potty training. They stop wanting to use the potty and tell you they want to wear diapers again or whatever. But Mars took it a step further and he did so during timeouts. He used his new super powers of pulling off his own pants, coupled with his newfound ability to control urination, to show us just exactly how he felt about timeouts. All over the floor, my mother's couch, my father's bedspread, and his bedroom. This was more frustrating than I'd anticipated. It's one thing when your child throws fits. Screaming and throwing himself on the floor is a thing I was prepared for. And it mainly effects the parent. But when the kid did something to MY parents, well… it was suddenly a different beast.

So potty training went on. And on. And on. And the problems stopped being about pee and became controlling his poop. He held it sometimes and sometimes he couldn't hold it. Once he got mad and pooped in his underwear and then didn't know what to do with the amount that got on his hand so he wiped it on the wall. **An Aside: I not-so-tactfully made my husband clean that up, because his mother told me he had also gotten poop on the wall as a child, meanwhile I have never done anything of the sort, except that one time in college when I got drunk and thought it would be funny to pee on a fire hydrant and discovered exactly why that was a terrible idea. It sprays. Gross, right? But not as gross as poop on the wall. Aside over**

Mars started hiding his pooping too. This was a control and shame thing which is a pretty horrible combination, because it means your kid is trying to control a bodily function when his world feels like he can't control it, *and* it means he's also ashamed about it. "World? I can't control that! Instead I'll pick stopping my poop." It's just awful to try to figure out how to fix a thing like that. And for me, who had worked with abused kids, it was a trigger, it turned out. It upset me in a profound way and I felt like I was failing, in a deeply fundamental and important way. As a bonus, I was also afraid of how his problems would be viewed. I don't know exactly who I thought would be viewing his problems but whatever. The point was, I was used to this particular problem coming up in relation to kids who had no control at home OR kids who had been abused. And the fact that my own child was doing this, despite being given plenty of choices and having zero abuse history, well - it was confusing. I swallowed my pride, though, and asked for advice.

The nonprofit where my husband worked at the time sent parenting experts into homes to help new parents. I asked a trusted parenting expert what to do with Mars' controlling pooping thing.

"Throw poop parties."

"I don't want him to *throw* poop! That's the only thing that's worse than what he's already doing!" I said in sleep deprived, coffee-laden tears that may have sounded more like "MBBBEEEAar…it's so hard."

She clarified that she meant to back off of the potty training part and focus on the pooping. She assured me that celebrating every time someone pooped was a good idea. I involved Mars in diaper changes with Gomez, thus reviving our mutual love of Beyoncé and shaking our butts, not to mention Gomez's, as soon as he was clean.

"If you like it, then you better put some cream on it," we sang to the tune of "Single Ladies." "If you like it then you better put a ring on it," are the real words. It came out in falsetto and we danced away the day.

I tried my hardest not to shame Mars when he had accidents that seemed intentional, although I wasn't perfect at this and I'm sure my exhaustion at the two children who were keeping me up at night and making me into a sleep-deprived loaded gun made it worse. But we threw poop parties. When I pooped, when Gomez pooped (which was approximately seventeen times a day), when Mars pooped. Yes, even in a public bathroom like, say, Target. Literally anyone. Strangers. We praised strangers for their pooping by whooping.

My favorite thing that I relearned during this time was how funny farts are. I had forgotten. In women's restrooms, there's an unspoken rule that you do not laugh when a woman sits down on a toilet and farts. Which happens constantly. Women don't ever fart out in the world, instead they hold it in, hard. Then as soon as they set 'er down on the toilet, they all fart. And no one laughs. Because there's a code about how the bathroom is a safe place where a woman is allowed to fart. Which is weird when you think about how loud some of the rips really are. But with Mars, all those farts were new again and he laughed so hard, I lost it too. And we threw poop parties and laughed at farts in Target bathrooms, and grocery store bathrooms, and the library bathroom, and of course at home.

I'm pretty sure we yelled "POOP PARTY, POOP PARTY, POOP PARTY, POOP!" at the cat as she was leaving her litter box once. This was helpful. Mars stopped hiding his pooping. But potty training took a very long time. And it was more stressful than it should have been. And his accidents were not met with the calm kindness they should have been, because they were more intentional than accidents. And if we'd waited until he held up that sign on the highway, it might have all gone easier. Even if I would have washed all the skin off my hands first.

At 3 Mars learned three lessons the hard way all in one day:

1. Don't touch that; it's hot
2. Don't pretend to bite your brother. He won't understand and he'll actually bite you.
3. Never trust a fart.

After the third thing when I told him to be careful farting, he said, "Yeah, because of my diarrhea, my farts are poopable."

Chapter 21

If You *DO* Push Potty Training, Try These Tips

If you DO push potty training, this is good info:

#1 Some children do *not* need help learning to pee outdoors. Specifically, my two boys did not need help learning to pee outside. This was a bit of a revelation for me.

I am a girl, and an outdoorsy one at that. And so I have peed outside a lot. I also had to be encouraged to do this as a little girl. I remember fighting and crying about NOT wanting to pee outside for fear of someone seeing me. I did not want to pee outside because it was yucky, I could not wash my hands, and someone might see me. If they saw me, I would surely turn to dust immediately. Or worse, I would survive in a world where someone saw me peeing. The irony of now living in a home with two little boys and one bathroom is not lost on me. I've come a long way.

One time, when I was eleven, my grandmother refused to find a gas station for me and pulled over in a field instead. She and my cousin both assured me that I would not be seen, as we were in the middle of nowhere. No sooner had I finished peeing and stood up, than a hundred bikers, black leather jackets and all, came thundering through, revving their engines and hollering at me. It was horrifying. That I did not turn to dust was a clear indication that a miracle occurred. It took a lot of time and alcohol and love of outdoor activity to reattempt outdoor peeing.

And so, I thought kids had to be encouraged to be comfortable with their bodies and bodily processes. This, it turns out, is a total girl thing. Either that, or I've been way too successful in this area. Because my boys did not need to be encouraged to pee outdoors. One time we had to pull over on the way to the airport and let the boys pee on the side of the road. They found a broken-down TV and giggled and peed all over it. It gave me renewed hope in "coallective competition" (the concept that we compete better together, you hippie). A better pissing contest with more winners was never held! The boys had a fabulous time, no one had an accident, and I made my flight. Winners all around! My boys love to pee outside and don't really mind pooping out there either.

#2 Don't try to get your kids to go in a Port A Potty or an outhouse until their potty training skills have completely set and become totally ingrained. We tried to take Mars and Gomez camping when Gomez had just potty trained and it nearly unpotty-trained him. He was cool with pooping in a hole but a Port A Potty? No thanks. He'd rather poop in his pants.

#3 Sing songs. I sang songs about all kinds of things. But especially about potty training.

When potty training Gomez, I whooped my own rendition of "Who let the dogs out? Poop—poop, poop, poop."

It, coupled with seemingly months of naked butt-time at home, combined for success in potty training. And Mars had felt similarly when he was about that age. One time when Mars was two, we went to the city, which is at a lower elevation than where we live, which means it's not snowy there when it's snowy by us. So we went to check out the snow-free parks and go swing and such. Mars was all, "Mom, I don't like the city."

"Why not?" I asked.

"There's goose poop everywhere. You won't let me be naked. And I have to pee in a Port A Potty. Can't I pee on the grass?"

"No, Mars."

"Yeah, I don't like it here."

#4 Be careful with the naked butt approach to potty training. Naked butt potty training probably has some en vogue, posh, Pinteresty name now but I don't know what it is. I potty trained my kids by letting them be naked a lot. They had easy access to the potty and used it. I started with a timer and asked my kiddos to sit on the potty whenever the timer went off. They gradually learned to hold it between and I increased the increments on the timer. Then I put their pants back on.

The first day the snow in the yard melted the spring that Gomez finished potty training, I forgot about sunscreen for his boy parts. We'd been doing naked time indoors because… snow. Plus, oh my God, the end of diapers is in sight! But with the snow suddenly and finally gone, the kids were excited to get outside and play in the yard. So we continued the naked butt theme, and he sure enough, got the same sort of sun burn you can get on your lips, uh…elsewhere. Poor baby. Be careful with the naked approach to toilet training. But other than that caution, it was a good way to go. Gomez potty trained quick and had no regressions.

#5 Plan for A LOT of extra time on trips. I mean every trip everywhere. Walking a block to the park is a trip. Any grocery store run is a trip. Before potty training little kids, I had never seen the inside of a grocery store bathroom. Now, I have a sixth sense about which corner of the megastore will have what kind of bathroom.

#6 In an online moms' group recently, a mom posted a question about what kind of undies to get for beginning toilet training with her young and very slight daughter.

My answer was "don't worry too much if the undies are too big. She's going to decide the best thing ever is wearing both legs through one leg hole, or wearing them backwards, and throw a fit if you try to convince her the Disney princess goes on her butt.

"Mommy, I can't fawt on Elsa!" or some such thing. Which undies don't matter so much as having LOTS of pairs for a while because if she's picky at all, she'll not like it when a single drop of pee drips in them and have to immediately change. Also, she'll likely have one pair as the only pair she wants to wear. She'll be getting her strongest opinions along with her ability to decide when to wee (exactly after you've gotten into a traffic jam.) You won't care though because EFF DIAPERS!!! Best of luck to you, smiley face.

I stand by that advice.

Gomez learned toddler first aid one morning. First, you pretend to burn your foot, then you take your sock off and apply copious amounts of chapstick, then you seek mom's help in putting your sock back on.

Then Gomez held up a finger, “I’ve got a bean in my bandaid and I have to put it in the box or it’s going to miss its friends.”

Meanwhile, Mars wears gardening gloves at the breakfast table.

Chapter 22

Surgeries

Pooping is normal and it happens a lot and you get used to it with parenting. There is more grossness and weirdness to parenting though than just potty training and poop.

"Mommy. Mo-mmy." The whiny two-year-old voice was gathering strength. I could hear the volume picking up from Mars' room.

It was still pitch dark out as I groaned and considered turning over and the effort it would take to move the cat, the covers, and my enormous pregnant body. At nearly eight months pregnant, starting my day was getting harder and harder. I considered briefly, but not for the first time, that surely this child was sent to destroy me. I got up and took a moment to collect myself in the bathroom before going in to get him.

"Coming, baby."

Mars heard the water turning on and off and quieted.

I exhaled and opened his door.

"It's still sleeping time, baby."

"No… no Mommy." He whined desperately. He was searching, "I need go bafroom." This was before potty training. He didn't use the potty yet and hadn't shown any interest. So it was a good way to get my attention, I thought.

"Listen, baby, it's still dark out and you need to get more rest. Mars needs rest; Mommy needs rest; Daddy needs rest. So I want you to stay in your crib and lay back down." Instead he stood up.

His pleading was getting to me and I resolved not to pick him up, but then I saw a dark spot on the sheets in the glow of his nightlight. I reached my index finger down and touched it. It was wet.

"Mars, did you get a bloody nose?"

I walked to the door and switched on the light.

Adrenaline thundered through my body at the scene. There was blood everywhere. I immediately knew why but it didn't stop the sight from upsetting me. We'd recently been to Mars' 2-year-old well-child visit and the doctor had warned us to leave the then-tiny, bright red mole beneath his eye alone. She'd warned us that messing with it would result in a lot of blood. My husband has bright red moles just like these and they're the size of a pinprick. You'd hardly notice them. But then in the last few days, Mars' had grown sizeably. It had clearly burst now and she was completely right about the amount of blood. There was a blackened clot the size of Mars' eye socket, partially congealed to his long eyelashes, and smearing down his cheek. Bright red covered half of his face. A puddle the size of a sleeping cat lay pooled red on the white sheets obscuring the pastel butterflies. I reached for him. I kissed his soft blonde head over and over again, his body cradled against me. I wondered if I did this to calm him or me.

"Rob!" I called out, doing my best to conceal my panic. I do not holler to wake people. I go to them and gently wake them. Always. I hate to wake people. Yelling for him meant it was serious. "Get me some wet wash cloths and a towel."

My husband walked in and surveyed the scene briefly with an Emmy-deserving poker face, before setting to work cleaning up the blood on our son's face. Remember when I said sometimes it's good to have a poker face? This was a good time for Rob's. I carried Mars into the bathroom, shielding his face from his own terrifying reflection. There, I held him, sitting on the toilet seat lid. I couldn't look at all the blood. I just kissed his head while Rob wiped and rinsed the washcloth repeatedly. I held on and kissed his head. "It's okay, baby. Mommy and Daddy are here. You're safe. We'll take care of it." And more kisses and more kisses and more kisses.

We spent the morning cleaning up blood and indulging Mars' every whim. He got to watch television while eating yogurt with bananas and blackberries on our bed (eating on the bed was not permitted but this was a day for breaking rules). One of us sat with him holding a washcloth beneath his eye, waiting for the bleeding to stop while the other rinsed and washed bloody bedding, cleaned the walls, the whole mess.

His doctor got us in right away and was a calming (NOT FREAKING OUT) presence, which was important. But she was not comfortable repairing or cleaning the wound both because it was so close to his eye and because, as she put it, "These things bleed like stink." Yes, I knew that firsthand now. Instead she called over and got us an appointment at the dermatologist for that afternoon.

The pretty young Asian doctor who saw us smiled and offered a delicate handshake before telling us "it needs to come off."

I stared at her smooth complexion the color of brown sugar and thought, "This was why she became a dermatologist - her stunning skin." I took in the details of her as though they might take away the idea of a bleeding eye. Her face was framed by long, dark hair. She wore carefully applied dashes of mascara and red lipstick. I shook my head back to what she was telling me. She nodded vigorously and repeated again and again how "it needs to come off." But she wasn't exactly sure how since he was only two and it was so close to his eye.

In the flooding of nurturing instinct and my self-distracted staring at this too-pretty doctor, I nearly missed the word "melanoma" as it left her mouth.

"I'm sorry, what?"

"We just want to rule out a melanoma." Then she added, "It's probably a pyronic granuloma, especially given how vascular it is, but I've seen melanomas recently in two different two-year-old patients that looked like granulomas so it needs to come off."

Absolutely right, without question, it needs to come off.

An image of my red-headed step-father's sun-damaged skin and him shriveling from melanoma in his chocolate brown La-Z-Boy slipped into my mind and I couldn't reconcile it with my blonde two-year-old sitting on the floor in flashing Spiderman tennis shoes and a red shirt with a crab flying a spaceship on it. His skin was so smooth, so perfect, so *not* sun damaged. I focused on "vascular" and "granuloma." I thought about going to Children's Hospital and wondered whether they would merely sedate him or completely put him under for the procedure. I nearly hyper-ventilated at the thought of him intubated.

"They'll let me be with him the whole time though, right?" As though if I held him through it all, it would protect him in some way that decades of research and training of the professionals in the room wouldn't.

As I drove us home, Mars noticed the traffic lights more than I did.

"Green light go, right, Mommy?" He'd learned about green and red lights in a single short drive two weeks prior and had been captivated ever since.

"Huh?" I'd been thinking of when he was newly born. I'd looked down at him while I nursed. I could see the capillaries in his ears through his translucent skin and I'd wondered at the perfection that my body had made. The thought had occurred to me in that moment: "One day, he will have a scar." It was a revelation and it broke my heart. This perfect body, this healthy, perfect body - he would one day probably put drugs and alcohol in it, or would play too rough and get a scar.

I snapped back to, realizing what he was talking about. "You got it, baby. Green light is go. You're so smart!"

And for a few moments he focused me and we talked about stopping and going and the lights. But then my mind went back to wandering. It would not be drugs and alcohol or a bike accident that gave him the first scar. It would be this surgery and it would be on his beautiful face, his large pooling dark blue eyes would be marred by this scar. I thought of the sunburn he once got when I missed a spot with the sunscreen just under his eye. Was it his right or left that happened to? My husband swears it was he who was responsible for this and to this day faults himself for the mole and the surgery; meanwhile, it had also been my response to take the blame. Parental guilt isn't reserved exclusively for us moms, it seems. We're both sure we forgot the sunscreen.

We soaked Mars in the tub in order to get the last of the crusted blood off before applying Vaseline to keep it from itching. There was the very gross and practical reality of cleaning up all that blood and we didn't want to repeat it. Mars played with his rubber Star Wars toys in the tub. Yoda zoomed around the beige tiles above his head.

"Yoda fying around. Darf Vader freakin' out."

Darf Vader and Mommy both, kiddo. And yes, that is an accurate definition of "freakin' out."

We missed the first surgical appointment available because there was a blizzard. Then I gave birth to Gomez and then I got a uterine infection after giving birth to Gomez so that put it off a bit more. Gomez was just a couple of weeks old when we headed to Children's Hospital for the first time one of our kids had surgery. Unfortunately, it wouldn't be the last, even though cancer would be ruled out.

The morning of the surgery, Mars was excited about his special event. He didn't mind the mole or the bleeding or any of it, really. He'd left it alone during the day and when we made him sit still while we waited for the bleeding to stop, he got to watch all kinds of TV he'd never seen before. Up until then, he'd only really ever watched Sesame Street, which he loved. But with this bloody eye business, he discovered all sorts of new PBS shows. So the idea of surgery to Mars meant a neat outing, a chance to wake up early, lots of new people to meet, and a chance to watch things. There was no downside in sight.

He loved all of those things. New people? Yes, please. Get up at a weird time? How exciting! Watch TV from a metal bed? Heck yeah!

But then as the time for him to go into the OR neared, the doctors and nurses started coming in all gowned up and with masks on. I could see him tense up at their covered faces. Toddlers are particularly afraid of masks, a fact you'll see vividly illustrated on Halloween by certain screaming, bawling children. Mars was no exception. At the least, he was intimidated and uncertain of the doctors and nurses with their faces obscured. He hadn't tipped over into full-blown fear yet so I had to act quickly.

Thinking fast, I whispered in Mars' ear, "They look like that because they're super heroes. That's why they wear those masks."

"What are their powers?"

"They have the power to heal!"

So then he yelled at the next Operating Room nurse he saw, "ARE YOU LIKE SUPER HEROES WHO HELP KIDS?" and this secured him excellent care because everyone at the hospital found him charming and precocious.

Terror averted, he tromped off down the hall toward the OR, lifting a tiny hand to wave at me without even looking over his hospital-issued gowned shoulder to see if I noticed. And I cried. I was terrified but my concern was unwarranted. He was out before I knew it and we were home by the middle of the afternoon. The mole was nothing more than a run-of-the-mill, bleeds-like-stink, noncancerous pain-in-the-neck. But dang it was gross and scary. And only an introduction for us.

The next surgery would be on Gomez. At four months of age, Gomez spiked a fever in the middle of the night. As I mentioned earlier, Gomez got up to nurse quite frequently at night and that night was no exception. I lay him in the bed and felt the heat from his bed as I nursed him. I realized he wasn't just warm, he was warmer than he should be. Much warmer than he should be. I checked his temperature. It was 103. I called the doctor's exchange and waited. They told us to bring him to the ER so we did. They didn't do much in the ER other than settle our fears. They confirmed dosages for fever reducers that we didn't know we could give yet, gave him some, and when his fever responded, sent us home with an order to follow up with our doctor when the sun came up.

We went in first thing in the morning and the doctor had us follow up with a urologist, suspecting that he had a UTI. At the time, I didn't realize 1. That boys got UTIs, which is dumb because of course they can. But I had just known that they are a frequent problem in little girls and often have to do with taking bubble baths. And 2. I hadn't realized how serious a UTI in a young baby is.

At the specialist, they set up an ultrasound of his kidneys along with a test where they track the flow of urine using a type of x-ray. This was unpleasant for a baby to say the least. Babies don't understand being restrained and you certainly can't explain "sit still" to a four-month-old. Instead, I sang to him and kissed his forehead while simultaneously firmly holding him and trying not to cry out "it's not fair!" At the time, I'd thought it was probably just precautionary overkill. He'd gotten a UTI. Weird stuff happens.

The specialist showed us his findings that day. Gomez had a reflux disorder making the tubes that take waste from the kidneys to the bladder a two-way street where they should go exclusively one-direction. This made him prone to bladder and kidney infections, and, if uncorrected, would likely result in long-term kidney scarring and eventually kidney disease. The plan was to keep Gomez on antibiotics constantly for six months, and if we could avoid any more infections, check his reflux again to see if it improved. I hoped that it would, but it didn't. So just before his first birthday, we went back to the hospital for a major abdominal surgery to correct the reflux.

In that six months, Gomez had developed like it was a race. He took his first steps at seven months and was skillfully up and down stairs by eight months. By the time he went into surgery, he'd been walking for nearly five months. So, despite the nine tubes and wires coming out of him (one of which was an epidural) and the two nurses it took to move him, he stood up and tried to walk. I hadn't realized how serious the surgery truly was until he did that and couldn't, and got so upset. He wailed in pain. His body felt like lead and I couldn't even figure out how to hold such a sad lead pipe full of tubes and wires.

I'd thought of how well Mars had recovered and how minor his ordeal had turned out to be. So when Gomez was in horrible pain, to the point of receiving narcotics when under a year of age… well, it was terrifying.

For more than a week after the surgery, Gomez had drainage tubs that extended from inside his body, from his bladder, to a double diaper system we had to maintain. So we had one diaper against his body, then a second diaper where the drainage tubes drained. It took two people to change his diaper every time. One person had to hold him still and the other did the diapering. And even still, he managed to grab and pull out his own drainage tube.

It was stressful, but the worst part was trying to get a baby to eat who didn't feel good. He'd been a picky eater, but an avid snuggler and loved milk. After the surgery, he didn't want anything. There was no food that interested him. He wanted to be near me, but he didn't even want to nurse. This was frightening. I was so desperate for him to take in calories, so biologically obsessed, I pumped a bottle of breastmilk and added chocolate sauce. I cried when it didn't work. I was afraid because he was getting dehydrated at the time and hydration is so important for recovery.

In all reality, he was fine and when he felt better, he got back to eating and drinking. And if he *had* gotten too dehydrated, they would have admitted him to a hospital where he would have gotten an IV to hydrate him. And that would have sucked but it also would have worked. I couldn't maintain that perspective, though. I was too afraid. Part of me knew and could hold onto that thought, but not all of me. I was too scared to completely trust rational thoughts or steps.

I don't have great tips or jokes about this time in our lives. It was scary but I did believe the whole time that it was temporary. It made me truly appreciate a healthy child and how lucky I was that this was temporary. I also had a dear friend who came to visit immediately following the surgery. She'd scheduled the trip before the surgery was set and we thought we were going to sneak off to ski, but instead, she helped with entertaining Mars and changing diapers and holding my hand while I cried in fear. She hung out with Mars while we took Gomez to the doctor to see if he'd need to be admitted for dehydration. She helped us cook and manage life. There is absolutely no better friend I could have asked for than this woman who helped us through that week of terror and mayhem. It was beyond stressful and she made it manageable. If your kiddo ever has to have surgery, I hope it was like our first experience and not like either of the two after.

By the time Mars turned four, my mom brought up her concerns about his sleep. She would occasionally have Mars spend the night with her. She did this because of how sleep-deprived I was. She helped this way to get me some relief, and she did it because she's a smooshy, mooshy gramma who loves that grandson and sleepovers.

After one particular night at her house, she told me she was worried about Mars' snorting and snoring in his sleep. I listened and looked into it medically. As it turned out, Mars had such swollen adenoids they were basically nose plugs. Those plugs resulted in sleep apnea which was why he'd wake up in the middle of the night. This was during the games of non-sleeping musical beds and sleep-chasing idiocy. We were way too exhausted to take note of the noises Mars made when he slept. We were so exhausted we took whatever time he slept gratefully and conked out ourselves. So thank goodness my mom noticed. By the time my mom brought these concerns to me though, Mars had been getting up periodically for about a year with a combination of night terrors and nightmares. Nightmares and night terrors can be indications of a medical problem but I didn't know that. I did know them to be normal for 3-4 year olds. At that age, children's imagination and language development are kicking things up. Kids are learning many, many words in rapid succession, and they're playing pretend a lot. So they're learning new words, reading books, and playing monsters and superheroes. All this causes some serious processing to go on in their sleep. Monsters...words! They really do have nightmares a lot at those ages, while processing through all that information. As a result, I hadn't thought too much of the nightmares Mars was having. I was exhausted and it seemed fairly normal. In all reality, he was probably choking and not breathing in the middle of the night and I imagine if you're processing through a new vocabulary and a big imagination in a dream when you suddenly stop breathing, you'd wake more than a little afraid. Possibly even terrorized, which may have explained the times when he woke up screaming. There was nothing you could do to comfort him, just wait until he calmed down which sometimes was as long as a half hour. And a half hour doesn't sound like much until you're holding a kid in terror.

So when Mars was four, his adenoids and tonsils were removed. After the diagnosis but before the surgery, I slept with him so he would wake up and have me right there to reassure him. It also helped him to know that I was there all the time. He still woke up, but it was less scary and for a shorter time.

When he went in for surgery, I was nervous, but not too bad. It helped my nerves that I've had my own tonsils and adenoids out. I was also comforted by the fact that he was much older than either of the last surgeries. His body felt sturdier, more able to withstand something so routine.

So I was shocked in the recovery room to find him lose his desire to breathe and be held in what's called a chin-thrust by the nurse. This is no gentle hold. The nurse held firmly to his mandible while ordering me to hold the oxygen mask over his face. The nurse meant business with this hold. This hold is a nurse's way of unequivocally telling a body to "BREATHE."

Eventually he breathed on his own but it took a day or so for his pulse oxygen concentration to come up to normal and so we stayed overnight in a hospital. Again.

Then there was the two-week time period during which Mars recovered physically from the surgery. If you're not aware, children don't always show signs and symptoms of pain the same way as adults. As an adult, if someone asks me if something hurts, I answer "yes" and take more pain medicine.

When I asked Mars about his pain, he'd answer that it didn't hurt. He'd be irritable and pick fights with his brother and with me. He'd whine and grump and grouch. So then I'd put a pulse oximeter on him and his oxygen concentration would have dropped and his heart rate would be up. So I'd give him pain medicine even though he'd fight the idea, and then 20 minutes later everything would normalize. Parenting Mars, aside from teaching me a lot about embracing gross stuff like sprinted poop prints, and gory bloody scenes, has taught me a lot about looking for signs. Mars doesn't sense things in his body like other people do. He can intellectually disregard the sensation of being tired or in pain or hungry. I once took him skiing and he cried hysterically, screamed at me, and refused to walk, until he straight up fell asleep on the concrete walkway. He'd never once mentioned being tired. He simply doesn't detect discomfort the way I, as an adult, do. I've learned to go through a checklist of what can be wrong when he's acting ornery. I consider when he last ate, pooped, slept, and whether something might hurt. I try to teach him to detect these sensations and I spend time with him when his body is all set with food, water, and rest to remind him of what it feels like when everything's good. It's finally working but this surgery was a help in dealing with a major problem we didn't know was happening: a lack of good sleep.

The entire ordeal of my mom mentioning her concern, the evaluation, the surgery, and the recovery was probably only six weeks. However, amidst those six weeks were my first book's launch party and several events related to it, and I was sleeping in a bed with Mars through every nightmare. It was intense.

I'm glad I could comfort Mars through all the fear. It's hard to get woken with nightmares but it's also one of the gifts of being the mom that you can comfort like none other. There's something nice about sleeping with your child right there and knowing you can help. I know an age will come when it doesn't work that way anymore.

After years of not sleeping, I'll never forget the feeling of walking into his room when I finally got him back in his bunkbed by himself after his recovery, and listening, and hearing nothing. The peace of all that nothing was a relief like none other.

After years of not sleeping and night terrors and hours of being awake while he played, he slept. His inaudible breathing was the best sound I'd heard from him since his first cries. It was wonderful.

And we are now, fingers crossed, done with surgeries for a while. I surely hope.

Mars (age 5) in a restaurant booth: "I'm going to love you respectfully from my seat, mom."

Chapter 23

Humping the Nap Mat

When I was pregnant with Mars, I listened to a lot of conjectures and reactions to his gender. We didn't find out ahead of time so people were always gazing at my belly and guessing at what was inside. I noticed a pattern of teasing the dad about having a girl. The ever-present fear being that one day a girl will date, or worse, have sex. This girl who has yet to be born. Yes, let's be scared about an unborn baby having sex. Right. Honestly, your concerns should, at this point, be about birth and getting the infant to survive the first few years of life…see also the previous chapters. It's harder than I thought.

As a woman, I found it irritating that someone would be so worried about having a girl. A little of me took it personally. So I did some soul searching and sure, you can get worried about having girls. But the reason to be worried about having girls has to do with figuring out where she might store her shoes, worrying about whether she will roll her eyes in middle school so much that someone might smack them out of her head, and worrying about all the awful ways other girls would treat her. The reason to be worried about having a girl would be because of the likelihood she'd be passed over for a promotion. I'd worry whether she'd be told by some pastor (yes, this happened to me) that people will assume she's flighty because she's pretty, when she herself hasn't yet noticed that she's pretty. She shouldn't need to notice yet for crying out loud!

The reason to worry about having a girl is that she'll be told to abide by a dress code which has more to do with controlling boys' behavior than anything wrong with what she's doing, and that teaches body shaming. Worry about body shaming. Worry about where to put a lot of hair ties. Worry about how to get poop out of all the fat and labia folds of a girl's parts. I honestly don't know how to do that. It looks gross; and shut up, I don't mean that in a body shaming way. She's a baby with doody all up in her theoretical labia. That is decidedly gross.

Anyway, boys are the least of a girl's concern. So she has sex someday. That's a bad thing? It'd sure be weirder if she *didn't* have sex one day.

My husband had this argument once with a coworker. She said, "I have a girl; you have a boy. You only have to worry about one penis."

And he replied, "Yeah, but do you know how much trouble one penis can cause?"

I'd argue they're both misdirected. I think they meant the trouble a penis can cause, in the reproductive department, but that's not the worst thing a boy does with his penis. Boys wipe and rub their penises on things. Mars and Gomez once had a literal pissing contest on our electric baseboard heater in the bathroom. It took me a week to figure out why I couldn't get the bathroom to stop smelling like pee, especially when it was warm in there. I have some idea of the trouble two penises cause and their penises and girls' vaginas are not what to worry about.

I have boys. Want to know what I worry about when I get ahead of myself and worry about the future? That they'll be like the boys I knew growing up, or like me. Or worst still, they could be some perfect storm combining those things.

I am a thrill seeker. I have jumped off cornices and rocks and cliffs on skis. If I'm hanging out with my skier friends and there's a diving board, I'm going to get all bruised up trying to see if I can learn to do a double front flip (I can't). As a teenager, I had guy friends who took acid and tried to bury the needle on their parents' cars.

THESE are things to be afraid of. Because these do not mean early movement into the grandparent category. They're things you *die* from. I'm not looking forward to having teenaged boys. That may be the point where I have to be put on a daily dose Lexapro for anxiety. I'll get through it though. I'll have conversations with my boys about sex and drugs and we'll be okay, especially if they don't drop acid or hang out with drug dealers. *I* hung out with drug dealers. My boys will do sports and not hang out with drug dealers.

These are the things I tell myself, anyway. They will do sports and not hang out with drug dealers. They will do sports and not hang out with drug dealers.

I've realized a lot of other parents don't tell themselves any of this, though. They worry about their kids having sex instead of accepting that this is a good outcome for their children's future. Especially in the US, where we parents are overwhelmingly unprepared to support sexual development.

If you're normal you're either flipping to the next section or cringing in preparation for reading about sexual development. Yes, sexual development. It does not start in the teen years. It starts when they're humping the nap mat in preschool. Yes, gasp all you want, but that is normal. Ask preschool teachers. They'll tell you about how many kids at naptime are having special alone time.

Tonight at bedtime, and often lately, a certain toddler in my world has been touching himself. This is normal. And I know that. And I tell him in the same tone I tell him to brush his teeth or to stop licking the cat, "You can touch your penis but that's something you do during alone time in your bed or in the bathroom." And he toddles off to the bathroom to go potty. For the third time in the last 20 minutes.

This part I'm prepared for, comfortable enough with, fine with. What I'm not so sure about and I'm relatively sure you aren't either is the time when I catch my kids touching each other's wieners, or worse, a friend is over and they play doctor. This is also normal sexual development. I want my kids to have healthy sex lives later. I want them to like sex. I am not afraid of my teenager being gay or having sex. Those things are fine and normal and have healthy, normal, predictable outcomes. I get grandkids out of those, or a son-in-law. More boys? Sure, why not.

(Which, as an aside, being a grandparent sounds like the best parts of being a parent but without the excessive amount of laundry. I hate the six-loads-a-week crap we do now but I love, love, LOVE spending my time doing puzzles and snuggling in for nap time. Aside over.)

When I add your kid into the mix of normal sexual development before the teen years, I begin to lose confidence in my devil-may-care attitude.

If you have any advice about this, please seriously do email me, especially if you're also the sort of parent who wants her kid to grow up to like sex. If you're some religious zealot who wants me to stop swearing and stop writing about kids humping the nap mat, take a biology course and grow up.

While I'd take any advice thrown my way about fostering healthy sexual development, I have some to offer about unhealthy sexual development. I've worked in child welfare and I've taught sex offenders.

I'm not an expert but I'm happy to share the information I've gleaned over the years. It appears to be information that nearly everyone in child welfare knows and that very little of the general population knows so here you go.

First a disclaimer: sexual abuse is NEVER the fault of the victim. Don't blame the victim.

That said, in children, there are some things you can do to make your children bad victims. Remember that the people doing bad things to kids know what they're doing and they do choose their victims so set your priorities on protecting your kids. Be more worried about a creepo grown-up touching your kid than worried that fifteen years from now she'll have sex. If you get a weird feeling from another grown-up, trust that and don't leave your kid with him, even for a moment. This is largely based on the training and experience I gained working in child welfare. I also used to work in a treatment center that dealt with a lot of sex offense specific behavior. So I've interviewed kids a lot, worked with kids who have been abused, and I've worked with teen sex offenders who were the ones who did the abusing. When I did that last one, I had no idea how many poorly written apology notes I could read that said things like "I'm sorry I stuck my hands in my pants during class. I promise not to stick my hands in my pants in class anymore." Offenders don't know squat about writing apology notes but they do know about secrets and choosing victims. Trust me when I tell you, offenders are savvy and you should prepare your children accordingly. Here are 3 practical tips on how.

1. Call body parts by their real names
2. No Secrets = teach kids you can always tell me
3. Teach kids to respect their bodies and teach them to do the same by example (no shame either, even if they've got doody in their lady folds)

What I mean when I say "call parts by their real names" is don't use baby talk words to describe body parts. Call it a penis not a woowoo or a fanzifuss. Call it a vagina not a woowoo or a fanzifull. If your child, heaven forbid, ever is touched, and they try to tell someone, no one will know what they're talking about if they call what was touched by a family-language specific name. If the kid tells someone that Bubba touched his hoozwallah, the person listening will think he has two stuffed animals named Bubba and Hoozwallah. I made this up, but you get the idea. If the person your kid tells *does* manage to understand what happened, that doesn't mean police or social services will understand when they interview the child. You may think this is overboard but I'm telling you that if I know this, so does a person who wants to do yucky things to children. They're savvy. Teach your kids proper names for their body parts.

I do this and I also teach my kids that no topics are off limits and that they can tell me anything.

No Secrets is a firm rule in my household. This may seem minor but again, perps are savvy creepsters who know how to pick a victim and how to convince a victim not to tell. They test it by telling kids secrets and seeing if the kid will keep a secret. You don't want your kids to keep secrets. The longer rule for us is "No Secrets, Only Surprises." This means that they'll still screw up a wrapped gift (a surprise, not a secret) by telling Uncle Joe exactly what's inside but they'll get the idea eventually. Surprises are fine to keep to yourself, because eventually Uncle Joe will be part of the surprise. Secrets are not okay because you can't talk to anyone about them. And there is nothing my kids can't talk to me about.

Perps tell kids terrible things like that their parents won't love them anymore or that their parents won't believe them and sometimes both and worse. Perps tell kids that it's their fault and that they're gross and the kids feel gross and so believe them and worry that their parents won't love them if they tell. You want your kid to be the kind who tells.

And if you've had lots of conversation with your kiddo around how nothing they could ever do would make you not love them and how there's nothing they can't tell you, they'll also tell you way more than you meant them to. On the way home from kindergarten one day, Mars told me about how he kept biting himself even though it hurt because he and his friend were pretending to get bit by imaginary invisible bears. He also told me how he licked his bites to make them go away and then he smelled himself. He tells me pretty often how many pieces of poop come out of him in the toilet. When he was really little, he once told me about sticking his fingers in his anus. I may have been a little too successful in avoiding body shaming but I'd take this over not knowing someone touched him in the huzafuzzle.

#3 Despite this previous example in which Mars bit himself until he got bruises all over his arms (kids just do so much weird stuff,) I have tried to impart a level of respect for their bodies in my children. This starts when they're really little with doing things like stopping when they tell you to stop while tickling. It also means that when Aunt Verna wants a hug but the 3-year-old says no, you go with the three-year-old and your own feelings about Verna get set aside. When Mars was three and we taught him the idea of his cousin's "bubble" AKA personal space, his response was, "I wish I could shrink myself so I could fit inside his bubble." This is normal, but you enforce respecting that personal bubble, from the inside and the out.

Well, geesh, that took a turn for the serious. Hopefully you stuck with it and got something out of it. And now I will tell you a funny story about a kid in normal sexual development and hopefully then you won't be too scared to let your children be in the world. And now for something funny.

When "Shannon" was three and at the peak of the nap-mat-humping phase of her development, her mother picked her up from gramma's house. Shannon was rubbing one out in the backseat and her mother said nonchalantly "What are you doing back there Shannon?"

"I'm cuddling my labia."

Shannon is a happy adult with a PhD. I hope she still cuddles her labia in her alone time. She is one of the few women I know who has never been sexually assaulted.

Gomez asked me to kiss his owie.

"Of course. Where?"

He lifted up his shirt, pointed to his nipple and said "on my polka dot."

Chapter 24

Mars & The Gay Penguin

It was the sunny week I was to start my freshman year of high school. My parents had been through a tumultuous few years. My dad had spent the last six months going to AA meetings and hiding in the basement on the computer with a 100-foot-long phone cord that stretched from his desk in one end of the basement, around the corner, to the laundry room where it plugged in and my dad was doing mysterious computer things that took up the phone line for hours on end. It would turn out to be the internet but I didn't know what that was yet. It was only 1993 after all. We still did our research papers using encyclopedias. My dad had started and stopped drinking a few times in the past few years and had been laid off from his corporate job. He'd now been sober nearly a year and had successfully landed a new job. He was packing up to move away from our suburban St. Louis home to somewhere in Chicago where he'd gotten a job. We were not going with him.

My mom had generally worn a scowl since this news was revealed. She was seemingly mad all the time.

Finally, a combination of teenage snottiness and disregard for decorum mixed with annoyance at her attitude. "What is your problem? You knew if he got a job somewhere else you weren't going to move. You *knew* he was moving. You chose this."

"I didn't choose anything. GEORGE!" she yelled to my dad. Then to me, "Get your brother and go downstairs. We'll be down in a minute."

My brother was playing guitar in his room. He was twenty and when he was home, he was always playing guitar riffs as fast as his spindly spider fingers could go, which was fast. His death metal band in Minneapolis had recently broken up and he was preparing to move to Colorado to be a ski bum. He emerged at my bequest and we all met on the black leather couch set my dad had purchased when he moved out two years before while my parents separated temporarily.

I was in shorts and the leather stuck to my legs. I peeled my skin from them and then sat on my hands and stared at the crests of white plaster wall texture and waited.

"What's her problem?"

My brother shrugged. "I don't know." He slumped into his seat and I did too. We waited until our parents came down to talk to us.

My dad came down first and sat in the stuffed leather chair to my right. My mom followed and sat across from him, her lips tight, jaw set. She was still angry. I rolled my eyes and waited. She gestured to him, and he began.

"Your mother's asked me to tell you guys what's going on."

"We know what's going on. You're moving to Chicago and mom's pissed and won't stop being mean about it all the time." I may have added that she just needed to get over it.

My mom sighed loudly; it could nearly have been called a huff.

"Well, there's more to it than that. A few years ago, when your mother and I split up, I had an affair." He paused and breathed in, steeling himself. "And it wasn't with a woman."

Now, my family is full of talkers and emoters. We are not reserved or soft spoken folk. We are loud and expressive. Quiet moments when there are two or more of us are rare. But this was a quiet moment. Silent, actually. This was by far, the longest silence in our entire family history before or since.

No one spoke for an eternity.

I had so many thoughts. He'd had an affair? Outrageous. This was shocking all on its own as I really did not think of my father, who valued honesty so highly, as someone who could do such a thing. And gay? That was so weird. I thought of nights at the dinner table when he'd be jovial and teasing. He'd make fun of fags and talk in a swishy gay voice to make us all laugh. He did another voice where he chewed his tongue and said "my name is Wilbuw and I can't tawk vewy good." Then in his regular voice, he'd retell the most recent joke he'd heard which was usually political.

I gathered other contradictions to his announcement. He had season tickets to the Hawkeyes football games and still made the drive to them regularly. I couldn't reconcile this image of my football-loving dad who made fun of fags, being gay. "Gay men don't like football," I thought. He's gay?

I thought of a poster tear-out that my brother had on his bedroom door for years. It had read "No Glam Fags." No one had balked at him putting this on his door.

The silence went on and on.

My dad began to fidget. His hands were folded and he wrung them loosely and shook out his shoulders. "Somebody say something. Tell me you love me, tell me you hate me, but please say something."

I was the first to pipe up. "Of course we still love you, but you cheated on mom? How could you cheat on mom?"

Before the announcement, I'd not accepted gay people. All I could think of was that watching two women or two men kiss was gross. But I also asserted that I'd sooner lick salty pavement as perform fellatio. I was sure I'd never do drugs, and wanted to be popular. I was young; my view was a skewed narrow slice. But literally, in the instant that my dad announced that he was gay, it widened. It needed to; it had been a mere pinprick. Like a frog at the bottom of a well, I could only see some of the sky. And I loved my dad completely. Of course I had to widen my view to include my dad into it. I had to make room for a new idea: that being gay was just fine.

I was still bewildered in the coming days as he loaded a moving van and drove away. And then as my brother also moved away to Colorado and I started high school. But over the next years, I went to pride fests and parades and gay AA meetings in Chicago and I got good with gay.

When I had Mars fifteen years later, I found a book called *And Tango Makes Three*. It's a book about a pair of gay penguins in the New York zoo who are given an egg which they hatch and raise AND it's based on a true story. Penguins are the symbol of optimism and have long been my father's favorite animal. So of course, I told my dad that he had to buy a copy and inscribe it for my kids. He listened and did it and all his grandkids have copies. So we own an inscribed-by-Papa George gay penguin book called *And Tango Makes Three* which I read at bedtime to Mars and Gomez. They've heard it enough times that they know all of the lines. Usually they're most interested in when they might be able to visit New York to see Central Park because there's a carousel and a toy boat pond there, both depicted in the book. But one night, Gomez took us in a different direction.

He kept turning to the page at the end of the book where the two gay dad penguins are there with their grown up, adopted, girl penguin daughter.

"Where's the mom? Is *that* the mom?" he asked, pointing to one of the non-gender conforming penguins. Just kidding. Penguins are a-sexual. No way, you just can't see their girl or boy parts. Seriously, who knows how to tell a girl from a boy penguin? Zookeepers and veterinarians but not me and not Gomez and probably not even the illustrators who drew them. Gomez wanted one of them to be a mom.

"There is no mom. There are two dad penguins."

Gomez was not satisfied and kept turning back to the page and wondering where the mom penguin was because clearly it was so ridiculous that there was no mom. And I don't know why on earth I didn't just point to one of the penguins and say it was the mom because really, who cares? I'm nearly incapable of lying, even when it's easier, even when it actually doesn't matter.

My honest response led to more questions which led to more questions, all asked by Mars. Gomez spent the whole time mad about the lack of a mom and then toddled off to flip the fish tank light on and off and on and off and generally mill about.

Mars asked, "How do two dad penguins have a baby?"

Me: "There are so many different ways to make a family. Some families are like ours where the mom and dad are married and have babies and stay together and others are your cousins, where the mom and dad were married and had kids and then split and now your cousins have a step-dad. So some families have a mom and dad who live together. Some have just a mom or just a dad. Some have extra grown-ups. Some have two dads."

"But HOW? *How* do two dads have a baby?"

Now, I have a few folks in my family who are staunchly opposed to adoption for some very personal reasons involving the 1960s and having babies torn from them, being called sluts, and not being allowed to keep their babies, so adoption for me is an even more complicated conversation than sex. So I opted for the non-conventional answer. Again, why don't I just answer with a lie? I knew what he was getting at. He wanted to know the logistics. He wanted to know where babies come from. I could have said they adopted but no. I didn't do that.

"Well, sometimes a couple of gay men find a lesbian couple and they work it out that way." I realize this is uncommon but thought it would get me off the hook for both the sex talk and the adoption talk.

It did not.

"But how, HOW? Wait, is this about The Blood?"

This is one of the many, many reasons not to live in a house with just one bathroom. I have periods. I know, you're shocked. Mars certainly has been. And I can understand that. It's unsettling when you stalk your mom in the bathroom, see that when she stands up there's a bowl of blood, pee, and toilet paper. Blood is usually an emergency indicator so I get it when the kids are worried about seeing it. And it's also gross. So Mars doesn't like it when I have The Blood and I don't either. I like it far less since I never get to pee alone and inevitably there's a pint-sized human asking about The Blood.

"Yes." I sighed and sat back to have the conversation. "The blood is when a mom doesn't have a baby and that blood would have been nutrients for the baby." And seriously, that's gross to tell a kid. And if you live with only one bathroom and if this means that your kids are aware of periods at an early age, expect them to be extra afraid of zombies and leery of babies. Because they both need blood to exist, zombies all the time, babies just early in gestation. But this was not Mars' first time having this conversation so he was focused on the issue of the gay penguin dads. He was uninterested in zombies and babies. Just babies.

Before going further, first I added a disclaimer. "Okay, Mars, here's the deal. This is not a secret. You can ask Mom or Dad or Gramma or Papa George about this so it's not a secret." I am consistent with my anti-secret policy. "BUT, you can't talk about it at school. I'm fine with you knowing this stuff but you are not to talk to other kids about it."

"Why?"

"Well, it's up to each family to decide when to talk about these things. So kids need to hear about this from their own parents and not other kids, so you are *not* to talk about it at school. Got me?"

"Uh huh." I could tell by how quiet his voice got, he had taken this information seriously. Which is good, because I really don't mind him knowing all about sex but I don't really want some other parent getting furious at me or my kid for having explained through a game of telephone my description of where babies come from.

"Okay, so there's always a mom and a dad. With the penguins it's like this: If a penguin mom lays more than one egg, she and that dad won't sit on both eggs, so one will die. So some mom penguin laid two eggs and wasn't going to take care of one of them. The zookeeper took the extra egg and gave it to the two dads and they sat on it and took care of it. With people, the lesbian moms can get sperm from the dads and then it goes into an egg and makes a baby."

"But where does the sperm come from?"

I exhaled and said, "From a man's penis."

"What?" He looked down, horrified. He gestured at his crotch, waving his hands outwardly. "How do they get it out of there?'

I then explained puberty. "You know how daddy has hair on his testicles and in his armpits and on his chest?"

"Yeah."

"Well, when you get to be a teenager, you will grow hair on your testicles, your voice will get lower, and it will start to feel really, really good to rub your penis. And some time you'll do that alone in your bed—"

"—I know, or in the bathroom."

"Yes. And it will feel good and then sperm will come out."

"What color will the sperm be?"

Purple with white polka dots. Rainbow turd color. Sprinkles will fly from your penis hole into a sunset. So, so many wrong responses.

I actually said, "You'll just have to wait and see. It's bedtime."

So then I told Rob what I'd done, and he was so thrilled he pooped a sprinkle. Really, not at all. He thinks my family's weird and he thinks it's weird that I tell Mars this stuff. You might too, but honest and open is what I believe in. Rob did admit that he doesn't want to have to be the one to have this type of conversation. So we made an agreement.

"You do the sex talks. I'll take drugs and rock 'n' roll," said Rob.

Sold. I am less than confident on my drug talk.

"Marijuana is good and fun but don't do it until your brain is ready when you're 25."

Yeah, doesn't that message just sing? Try again. Nah, Rob can figure out what to say that's not "marijuana's fun but don't do it."

Then the next day, I left the kids in the car with my cousin while I ran in to grab a few ears of corn to go with the freshly breaded, homemade fried chicken my mom was making for a family dinner that night. I returned to this.

Cousin Anna: "War."

Me, swinging my legs in and shutting the door: "Huh?"

Anna: "Mars asked about war while you were inside. "Is there a war now? Is there war here? Is there a war anywhere? Has there ever been a war here?""

Me, bursting out laughing: "Haha! I got sex. Rob got drugs and rock n roll and apparently you got war."

Anna: "Great."

There's so much gross and weird stuff involved in parenting.

One morning, Mars handed me a maxipad and told me it was cake. He obviously has a future in sales.

Chapter 25

Don't Put "Poop Pinata" on Your Grocery List

Like all highly distracted parents, I try to balance my attempts to remember things with the chronic problem of partially completing many things at the same time. I use lists to do this. Even if I only have a bit of three different lists on one piece of paper actually written down. See, that's how you partially complete things, you use partial lists! On the following page is an example with three lists on one page.

I knew what each of the items on each of the three lists meant, but had just jotted down some notes all in the one notebook I could manage to find. I used to make grocery lists on junk mail envelopes, and keep a notebook with writing ideas and journal jottings and poems by my bed, but I blame my children for the fact that I ceased that habit. I attempt to organize. They attempt to destroy. These things are at odds with one another, and my husband is on their side. See also, eating apples in the bathtub. My kids often scribble all over my notebooks and take them so I end up finding one with a blank page and it looks like this.

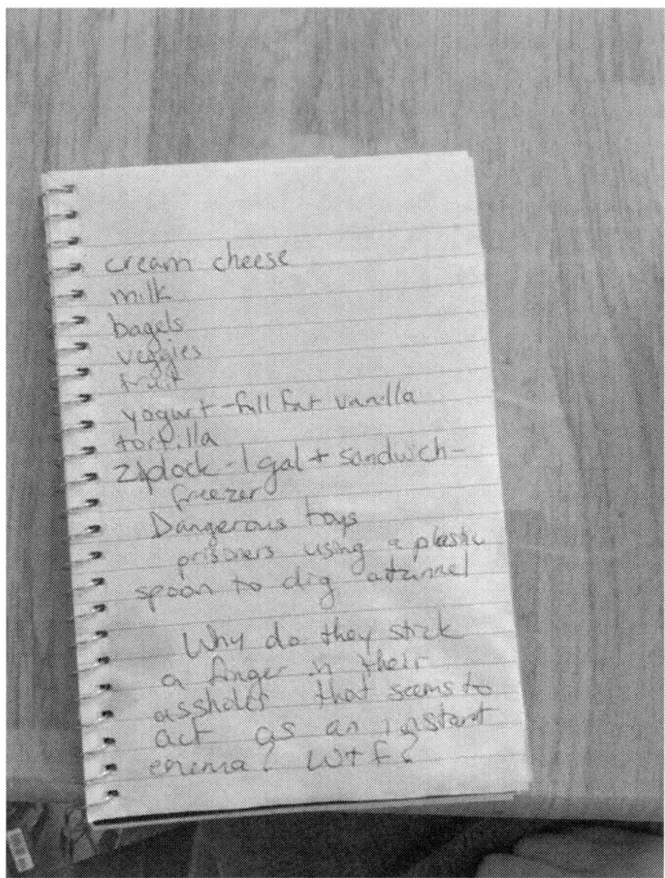

The list photographed says:

Cream cheese

Milk

Bagels

Veggies

Fruit

Yogurt- full fat vanilla

Tortilla

Ziplock- 1 gal & sandwich freezer

Dangerous Toys- prisoners using a plastic spoon to dig a tunnel

Why do they stick a finger in their assholes that seems to act as an instant enema?

My husband found this list when he was preparing to go to the grocery store the other day and understandably had questions. The top is obviously a half-start at a grocery list. It looks like my grocery list used to look when I was single. Svelte, simple, ending…this list encompasses what my single life was like. Simple, ending…because this list is only a tenth of what we actually buy and eat, I just make up the rest of the list in the aisle and keep going until I've spent at least $200 and feel like crying at the thought of unloading it all at home.

My list then continues on with dangerous toys. No, I don't need to remember to buy dangerous toys at the grocery store. This was because while I was making the grocery list, my husband picked up a toy that had no obvious small parts, but which boasted a label for age 3+. The sticker proclaimed that the item had small parts and warned of a choking hazard. It was a large, bright red toy microphone.

"There's no choking hazard here." My husband banged it on the table a few times forcefully to demonstrate his disagreement with the label. I was honestly more worried about our table collapsing and being a danger to the children than I was the toy having choking hazards. Much of our household is in disrepair and the table is no exception. Still, I decided his comment deserved an answer.

"You forget how kids have nothing but time to do what you just did, but for way, way longer. Think of how many things our kids have destroyed. They're experts at destruction. The company's right to have that warning. Somewhere in there are small parts and tiny hands will find them."

Toddlers have the focus of prisoners but use it to destroy a house or a bathroom or your notebook. So no, the toy had no obvious choking hazards. BUT, I pointed out, prisoners have been known to dig tunnels to escape using only a plastic spoon and a lot of time. Or maybe that's just in movies. I like movies. Whatever, I choose to believe that someone in prison really would and could do that. And toddlers and babies are just like prisoners. They would totally bang that toy for all the world like a prisoner until they found the choking hazard parts and then use them to dig to China. I *know* my kids have all the patience in the world to work at destruction, and digging to China. On a recent playground trip when I tried to take away their sticks so they didn't stab each other's eyes out, they screamed at me "but these are for digging a hole to China!" My three-year-old had already made a near-perfect circle and the interior plans for their hole were lain.

Obviously, I wanted to remember that toddlers are just like prisoners so I jotted down a note. Don't your grocery lists look like this?

Probably the point where it becomes off-the-charts weird is "why do they stick a finger in their assholes that seems to act as an instant enema?"

I concur. This was a genuine WTF note. Because WTF?

It's one thing when you have ***one*** kid that does this. I remember when my first stuck his finger in his asshole.

"Wash your hands," was all I said.

But he's a unique kid and I figured it would stop so that was my only response. Plus, he didn't hump the nap mat so I thought maybe that was his way of developing sexually. I know they're supposed to be developing sexually at that age so maybe that kid just did it by sticking his finger in his asshole. Freud's anal fixation or whatever. Maybe all of Freud's ideas weren't wrong after all. I also thought Mars was so pretty that maybe he'd grow up to be a fabulously beautiful gay man all handsome and stylish and quippy and I'd be the mommy version of a fag hag. So I considered the finger in the asshole thing a personality quirk or maybe an early sign he was gay. I doubt it now though. By now I've seen his response to women in bikinis too many times to think that.

But *then* the second kid did it too and made himself into a human poop piñata, so I made note. Like that tiny toddler finger was the final whack of the bat against the piñata and BOOM! The bathroom got poop all over the floor. And what the what??? Is it just a 3-year-old thing? Two kids doing this at similar ages would seem to indicate so. Nature or nurture? Nurture would imply that parenting or environment had taught these two that sticking fingers in assholes was a good idea and I just can't imagine what we have done that screamed out that message. Here's a small plastic knife to help me cut up your kiwi, oh and that's a hidden message that you should stick your finger in your asshole? I don't see the connection. So, that leaves nature. Nature seems weird too though.

I would be really surprised to learn that toddler me stuck my finger in my anus. REALLY surprised. I never ate mud, no matter who said it tasted however they said it tasted. I have never eaten paper. If you want me to smell something because it's gross, I'll tell you to eff off. So I just seriously doubt that I stuck my finger in my asshole. I'm pretty sure I humped the nap mat like other little girls. Maybe it's a boy thing.

Both my boys did this. When my second did this, thankfully it was in the bathroom and the cleanup was tolerable. Still, I probably didn't stay as cool as I did the first time with the first kid. I probably said something like "'the hell?" or let's hope it was just "REALLY?" And then probably some grumbling about it being gross and then this part I'm sure of. "Don't stick your finger in your butt." And then I had déjà vu and realized this was not the only time I'd told a three-year-old not to stick a finger in his butt.

That seemed noteworthy so I jotted it down…on my grocery list. So probably someone should tell me: no matter how many small children in your house, you shouldn't write "poop piñata" or "enema" on your grocery list. Parenting just involves so, so much gross stuff that you put it on the grocery list without a second thought.

PART FIVE
I Can't Blame The School

I tried to teach Mars to use the phrase "boldly forward" instead of "straight ahead." He was more successful with "damned car seat."

Chapter 26

Malefactor

At one point in the writing of this novel, I got panicked about having enough content. It's easy to jot down a funny quip and it's easy to tell stories at a party, but fleshing out chapters had been a lot harder than I'd anticipated. So I asked Rob, "What do you do with a fifty-page book?"

Without skipping a beat, he answered, "Set it aside and take notes for a few months and see what else they lick. Wait for an example of a time when they should have licked something but wouldn't."

Me: "—"

"Like for example this morning when Gomez should have licked the whipped cream off of his bacon but refused." He continued, "I've never seen someone wipe bacon on their shirt but there it was. Instead of licking it, he sure enough wiped it on his shirt."

At this point, Mars came in and sat on a yellow balloon.

"I sit on my pelota," he said.

"No es una pelota. Es un balon." I told him it was not a ball but a balloon. But my Spanish isn't amazing so I turned to Rob for assurance, "Balon, right?" Just asking the question convinced me that I had the right word so without waiting for a response, I went on. "Si. Un balon amarillo."

Mars patted his bottom and repeated "balon amarillo."

"No, that's your culo."

Realizing I may have just taught him a cuss word in Spanish, the first language of more than half of his school, I back pedaled. "Wait, is 'culo' a bad word or is that just butt?" I asked Rob.

"I think that's a bit rude."

"Wait, Mars don't say that, I think it's not a nice way."

"Culo?"

"Right. Don't say that one." I whispered, "I think it's like saying ass."

"Wait, what's ass?"

Oh god, what have I done?

I have had children, that's what I've done. And occasionally when I try to teach them something in a way that I *think* will be seamless, like throwing a Spanish vocabulary word in conversation, this is how it turns out. Other times I'm more deliberate with language.

Before kids, I loved, loved, loved to swear. It was probably a little too much to be honest. But swear I did. I had quite a reputation as a girl likely to use a large vocabulary that was heavily seasoned with the f-word. I never swore around the kids when I was a teacher, but the rest of the time, all bets were off. Especially at home in the evening *after* spending all day not swearing, my mouth would really be ripe for some zingers. I love language and I'm emphatic if not hyperbolic so I loved to get creative with my swearing. When I got ready for Mars to learn to talk, though, I figured I'd better clean it up.

Swearing is great in the adult world. It's trashy in kids. I don't make the rules but that one I follow. I have a strong aversion to anyone thinking my kids are trashy. They might get naked and put underwear on their heads, or rip off all their clothes to swim in a pond on a hike, but I make sure their nails are clipped and their socks match and that they wear clothing, not jammies, when we leave the house. All because I don't want anyone to think they're trashy. Also, it sounds awful when parents cuss up one side and down the next around children, and still worse when little kids repeat that stuff. I can't count how many times I was in a child welfare meeting where someone would describe something particularly grim or offensive that a kid said. Then someone else in the child welfare department would comment that the parents were clearly the source of such language. A you-know-where-he-must've-learned-to-talk-like-that sort of comment always followed.

In preparation for my own children going out into the world, especially into the world of public school, I wanted them to have good vocabularies. I wanted them to be polite, understood, listened to, well-mannered, and well-received. I had really high hopes and not swearing was part of them.

Learning to not swear at home was a transition and like the generations that precede me (i.e. replacing "son of a bitch" with "son of a gun") I came up with phrases to use to switch out. Instead of complaining about what that douchebag politician did, I said "that juicebag politician."

When Gomez was two, Rob taught him to say "malefactor." I hadn't thought of this as a sneaky and erudite replacement for saying "motherf#cker," but it is one. When Gomez said malefactor at two, let me tell you, it did not sound like "malefactor." I was there to witness Rob teach it to him though so I knew for certain how to decipher Gomez's utterance.

So I made my switches and stopped saying the f-word or the s-word at home and all around became Suzie Homemaker. Or something.

Unfortunately I was unable to give up the phrase "God damn it." And if you've read the previous couple of hundred pages, you know how often one might have said "God damn it," especially if that one was me. And since it was, I'm pretty sure Gomez's first sentence was "God damn it."

I come by this honestly. My mom, who has spent loads of time with my kids in a way that is so fabulous I don't know how anyone would do this without a gramma, also said "God damn it" a lot when I was a kid. She has modified that as a gramma.

This was a conversation between Gramma and Mars when Mars was two.

Gramma: "Dog gone it!"

Mars: "Sometimes you say 'dog gone it.'

Gramma: "Mmm hmm."

Mars: "Yeah. Other times you say 'shit'."

So we did our best to get rid of bad language and we did sort of okay-ish. Preparing to send my kids out into the school world proved to be very similar to telling them to stop licking things. It sounded simple. It has not been easy to pull off.

"Daddy, my teacher's like a cartoon. She never goes potty." Mars, about his Kindergarten teacher.

Chapter 27

Mars Wins at Kindergarten, or Something

I was so excited for Mars to go to kindergarten. The relief from childcare expenses sounded awesome. We live in a wonderful school district and I've spent a lot of time in our schools and know them to be good places for kids. I was over the moon. Still it was a new situation: new kids, new teachers, new scene. It represented a big change for us. So I was also nervous. Would his teacher like him? Would he be too young for his class since he just makes the age cutoff to enter kindergarten? Would he learn to tie his shoes? Would he be sad when all the other kids lost teeth before him?

Who he would befriend was not among my many concerns. Mars has always seen the world as a place full of friends he has yet to meet. I remember him having a problem with a big kid one time and telling me about it.

"The kid said he didn't like me."

"What? Why? What a jerk."

"That's not nice, Mommy. You shouldn't call him names. He's a nice kid. He just doesn't like little kids. But it's okay. I think I convinced him to be my friend by the end."

The kid can't be stopped. His response to someone not liking him is not to have his feelings hurt, but to take that kid's friendship on as a personal challenge.

And remember when he made friends with all the doctors and

nurses at the hospital by telling them how they had the power to heal? He's good at making friends. So I expected to hear about many classmates when he came home from school. I was not disappointed.

The first kiddo I remember him coming home talking about was a girl named Tortola. Yes, like the island where she was possibly conceived. Or maybe she's in the turtle dove family. Somehow I doubt it. She's pretty cute and definitely human.

Tortola was soon Mars' girlfriend and he talked about her constantly. After many times being warned about the constant affection they were showing, the two of them had to be limited to hugging just twice a day. They sat together at every lunch and I heard about Tortola at home constantly. When I'd pick him up after school, he would smile, start running toward me, stop and turn back, running to give one last vigorous hug to Tortola.

Ever since Mars was a little tiny thing, little girls have been coming up to pick him up and carry him around. And remember the Thanksgiving where he told that cute girl with the huge rack that he wanted to pour sugar on her and eat it? Yeah. So I was none too surprised when the first call I ever received from the principal was this.

"Is this Mars' mom?"

"Yes, why? Is he okay?"

"He's fine. He's just had some trouble at school today. It seems he and Tortola kissed at lunch." I stifled a laugh as he continued, "Apparently they made plans to get married at the Friday Fun Party tonight and when one of the boys told Mars he was going to tell on them, Mars told him 'No you're not or I'll punch you in the face.'"

I stood up and headed out of my office to continue the call outdoors where I could pace better. I walked around the block about three times as the principal and I talked.

"Oh no. Obviously, it's not okay that he said this. But I don't think he meant that he really would do that, it's something that he says, but I don't think he really understands the concept."

"I'll punch you in the face" is the only threat he knows. He actually didn't really know what a punch in the face was like (at that point) on either the giving or the receiving end. By now he does because Gomez has now punched him in the face. But then he didn't. So I doubt Mars thought the other kid would get scared or anything. He was speaking hyperbolically. I wonder where he got that? Still, we're not down with our kid making threats.

I got serious with the principal and asked what we as the parents could do to best support the school on this. We chatted and worked it through.

I flashed back to the first time Mars came home and cried in my lap after school.

"What happened?" I asked amid the squeaks and burps of the rocker we sat in together.

"There were these kids and they pulled this girl into the tall grass-" he turned to face me and gestured for effect, karate chopping his thoughts to show me where the tall grass was "-there's this tall grass over here-" chop "-and we're not really supposed to go there but these kids were pulling this girl by her hands and they pulled her into the tall grass. And I could tell she didn't want them to. I could see it on her FACE." He barely paused to breathe, he was so worked up. "So I told them it wasn't nice."

My heart had swelled with pride and I'd smiled. My husband runs a nonprofit, which would just days after this begin making their annual rounds of the local schools to talk about healthy relationships. The nonprofit is devoted to victim's rights and helping victims of domestic violence and rape. Their prevention groups at the elementary schools are called the Peacemakers and I definitely wanted Mars to grow into a charming little peacemaking, feminist and this was seemingly the answer to my request for such a child! We'd succeeded! His Montessori preschool was coming into play at the public school and he was choosing to stand up for a little girl. Big mommy gold star for me!

"But then they told me to mind my own business."

He was deflated and cried. She'd been fine and they'd all lined up to go inside but still, I was confident of his assessment that the situation was unwelcome. I was sad for him in his helplessness.

And now a short while later, he had threatened to punch a kid in the face if said kid told on him for kissing a crocodile. So much for my gold star.

I asked into the phone, "What did *he* say? Was he honest about what he did?" Honesty is big for me and it's hard at five. At five, some kids are lying a lot and telling what they want to be the truth and they've also got all this magical thinking going on and sometimes they get mixed up about what the truth really is. Still, I knew with this scenario that if he'd lied, he would need a serious lesson on lying because in this situation, he would know truth from not.

"He did tell me what happened honestly," the principal responded.

Whew, he'd been honest to the principal. That was good.

The principal continued, "I talked to Mars and told him about how important it is that everyone at school feel safe. And what he'd said didn't make the other boy feel safe at school and that's not okay."

I started and stopped a few lines of thought about how I would talk to him, about how we'd follow through at home. I wondered about whether I should follow through or if that would make too big of a deal out of it. Finally, I just asked. "What can we do at home to best support the school on this? Because I don't want to overdo it and overreact, but I also want to be sure to follow through at home to support what he needs to do at school."

The principal took a lot of time out of his day to talk to me that afternoon about what was an appropriate punishment, not too harsh or too lenient. We determined that this time, if Mars told me honestly what had happened and took accountability, no further punishment than what he'd had at school would be necessary. If he lied to me, he'd miss the party that evening.

At the end of our conversation the principal joked, "You're going to have your hands full with that one; he and Tortola are quite a pair!"

I still thought the kissing part of the first call from the principal was funny so I immediately phoned a girlfriend.

"Mars got called into the principal's office. Guess what for? He and his girlfriend made plans to get married after school and then he kissed her."

My friend and I both laughed.

"But then this kid told him they weren't supposed to be kissing at school and threatened to tell so Mars told him he was going to punch him in the face."

My friend said, "maybe the other kid deserved to be punched."

I make friends with seriously loyal people.

"Be that as it may," I responded. "Mars is not going to be able to pull off the threatening bully role, not long term. Seriously, look at Rob; look at me. There's no way Mars is going to be big. He's going to be small. Let's stick with prince charming, loverboy. Those he can pull off."

"Fair enough."

Mars was honest, albeit ashamed when he and I talked. Because he took full accountability, he still got to go to the school party. And as it would turn out, Mars and Tortola and his affinity for girls were the least of his kindergarten troubles. There was someone else heading our way.

The thing Mars was most excited about in kindergarten was riding the bus. And I'll admit that walking to the corner to drop him off and pick him up was pretty high on my convenience list as well. But still, I recall learning all the lyrics to 2 Live Crew songs on the bus. So I was watching out.

Mars' bestie in kindergarten has been this kid Keevine, pronounced Kevin. Mars began arriving home with small toys that Keevine had given him on the bus. After about the third time he came home with a small toy from Keevine, I told Mars it was time to stop taking gifts from Keevine. I didn't have a solid reason, but intuition told me you don't get something for nothing. I was right. We got so, so much from Keevine.

Keevine, aside from having a clearly mispelled name, an annoyingly popular destruction of the English language at its base, is a nice kid. Why do parents insist on naming their children normal names and then spelling like it's a creativity contest?

"This is my son Know-AH."

"Nice to meet you, Noah. N-o-a-h?"

"Close. It's spelled B-A-N-A-N-A-S."

I digress. Back to Kevin, spelled K-E-E-V-I-N-E.

If you sit across from Keevine at lunchtime, he is affable and smiles freely. I would find out firsthand what eating lunch with Keevine was like in a few months. But first, I had a few other Keevine lessons to learn.

The first was when I got my next call from the school.

"Can you come to the school to get Mars?"

I arrived shortly thereafter and found Mars, nonplussed, seemingly enjoying his time in the nurse's office. I exhaled my frustration and we stepped into the private restroom off the nurse's office to have a bathroom break and talk.

"I'll always come help you at school if you need it, but what's going on? You don't seem sick. I don't understand."

It seemed like maybe he needed to try to poop. That's a pretty common problem for kids when they start school. A lot of them get scared to poop at school. In Mars' case, he didn't want to miss class time and he also hadn't wanted a kid to stick his head under the stall door and see him. Which makes sense. There was a kid who'd been getting some big kindergarten laughs for doing just that. It would be unsettling to have someone's head appear under the door while you were pooping. But it also doesn't make sense in that Mars has peed on a TV on the side of the highway and has also been known to yell "POOP PARTY,

POOP PARTY, POOP PARTY, POOP!" in a public restroom. Still, school is a new setting that Mars was still figuring out how to navigate.

"Why don't you try to sit on the potty. You know, it's okay to take a break to go to the bathroom."

Once I'd settled down and Mars was sure I still loved him and he'd pooped, he let out the truth.

"There's a haunted tractor on the playground that drives on its own and will run you over and kill you. The field where it lives is full of skeletons and I'm scared it's going to run me over."

It would turn out that Keevine had told him all of this. I reassured him that the tractor was not able to drive without anyone and that Keevine was probably just playing make believe and had taken it too far.

"No, Keevine knows. He said it's real. He's not pretending. He told me!" Mars insisted.

"Well, sometimes kids your age get so into making believe, they get mixed up. I bet Keevine didn't know how scared you were. Let's ask Ms. Alice about it. She's been here since before the school was even built. In fact, she may have seen some of it be built and can tell us more."

We talked to Ms. Alice, the secretary and keeper of the elementary school, who said nearly verbatim what I'd told Mars. So I breathed a sigh of relief and he breathed a sigh of relief. Thank you, Ms. Alice. The tractor would not kill him.

But this was not the end of the fun with Keevine. It was a mere hint at it.

In October, the whole family took a trip to St. Louis to help promote my first book. I'd been invited to talk to my mom's previous church community. My mom had moved away a few years prior to this trip so she wasn't there. I'd brought Mars along because he loves church.

Mars had gone without me to Sunday school while I was the guest speaker in the adult forum. We met back up in the airy narthex with its high wooden beams and bright light.

"How was it?"

"Great!" he said, skipping toward me. "Can we get a donut now?"

"Yes!" I smiled and picked him up, hugging him in close and kissing the top of his head. "I need to gather my books and stuff. What's that?" I asked, letting him lean back so that I could examine the paper crunching against me.

I walked around, checking for his jacket and the bag and box I'd brought in with books supplies. I was half listening to his description of the Sunday school lesson and what the paper had to do with it all.

"I'll be right back," I told him and jetted the stuff out to the car through a side door.

I sprinted back to hear Mars in the narthex of the church say the f-word at the top of his voice, which can get quite loud. It was echoing.

You'll remember, I have a penchant for swearing. In fact, I love it. But since I don't love it coming out of the mouths of babes, I had put aside my significant love for swearing years prior because obviously, I love my tiny human offspring far more than the f-word. So I was flummoxed and more than a bit perturbed to hear the word despite the no-small-effort on my part to rid our household of it.

I knelt down and hissed to him "you are not to say that word at church!" I looked left and right to see who had heard. There was seemingly no one around by this time.

I rushed Mars to the car as quickly as I could. After what felt like an eternity, I finally had Mars buckled into his seat and I shut the driver side door, clicked my seatbelt into place and addressed Mars.

"Where did you hear that?" (Please don't say me, please don't say me). I put the car in reverse and headed out of our parking spot.

Mars from his car seat: "From Keevine on the bus."

Me: "Aha..."

I felt my anger rising but reminded myself of his age. I peeked at him in the rearview mirror; he clearly had no idea there was a significant problem with what he'd just hollered at the top of his lungs in the church. His car seat straps made him look so small and young. I wondered how he could say such things as I pulled out of the parking lot and began driving down the road.

Me: "Well, we don't say words like that in our house," (anymore, or if you're under 4 ½ feet tall).

Mars "Yeah, but..."

Me: "No buts. Do you like sitting with Keevine on the bus?"

Mars: "Yeah."

I gripped the steering wheel so tightly my fingers were beginning to tingle. "Well, if you want to keep sitting next to Keevine on the bus, I'd better not hear that out of your mouth again."

Mars: "Oh."

Me: "If I hear you say that word again, especially at church, I'm going to climb on the bus *with* you and talk with the bus driver about exactly what Keevine said and how you're not allowed to sit next to him anymore. Got me?"

Mars barely looked up and his eyes were big, yet unfazed by the conversation. "Uh huh. Do I still get a donut?"

Ugh.

Mars did better about the F-word for a while. It was another few months before it made a comeback. Mars then had said "fucking bitch" to his little brother when he was mad, which he'd again heard from Keevine but this time he'd heard it at recess so my threat to separate them on the bus didn't help. So then Gomez went through a particularly awful phase of repeating "fucking bitch" in the bathtub. Which was frustratingly a result of hearing Mars say that phrase which was frustratingly a result of Mars learning it from Keevine.

These conversations about swearing and confusions about make believe are likely common for kids riding the bus and going off to public school for the first time. I am okay with these conversations. I can grit my teeth and watch what I say and get through them. It sucks, but it's normal.

Then there are the other conversations. The other conversations have been about Keevine's religion. These are a new ballpark of conversation I hadn't much bargained on.

As Halloween discussions began in the weeks after the f-word in church incident, I was reminded that many of the students that go to Mars' school, practice a type of Christianity that believes that Halloween invites the devil to munch on your immortal soul.

"Keevine says Halloween's for the devil…" Mars waited for a response. This had been a question, apparently.

"Well, some people think that. But I just think it's for fun and dressing up and eating candy."

Mars wasn't convinced. I could see his worry so I repeated myself.

"Listen Mars, some people's families believe that's what Halloween is about, meanwhile we believe it's just costumes and fun." But we respect that they think what they think, blah blah blah.

I did not tell him that the down side to culturally diverse education is that whack-a-doodles overthink kids dressing up as monkeys and Iron Man or whatever. So what comes into play is that you have to deal with people who think the devil's around every corner waiting to suck your soul out your eye holes. Or something. But I didn't fall into that trap. I just said the culturally respectful thing and let my kid dress up in Iron Man's mask and furry monkey pants.

We had to have the Halloween religion conversation quite a few times though because Mars really was extra concerned by what Keevine said about how celebrating Halloween is evil and how the devil would attack him with a tractor and suck his soul out his eyeholes.

Come Halloween, Mars marched through the school in his monkey costume in spite of the devil, and he ate candy and enjoyed Halloween fine so I thought we were in the clear.

By this time, we'd stopped him from riding on the afternoon bus. My rationale was that hopefully the kids were too sleepy in the morning to get up to too much mischief and so Rob and I were taking turns picking Mars up from school. So no more toys were coming home from Keevine. Just the occasional comment about evil and the f-word from recess.

But then Mars started asking me "are we ready for the New World? Keevine says the world is about to end and that we have to be ready."

At this point, I thought lovely things like we can't even get ready for the next season much less then end of the world.

"If we can get ready for November, I'll worry about the New World." I tried brushing aside Keevine's comments about the end of the world but Keevine did not stop talking about the end of the world and so Mars, an anxious kid, was still worried. No idea where he gets that...see also chapter on anxiety levels and how I interpret my kid's behavior depending on my anxiety level, but I digress.

After Christmas, Mars got all upset about a sermon from Keevine about how Jesus held up one finger and the world ended. And that was going to happen again sometime around Thursday. And was Mars ready for the New World to come on Thursday when Jesus held up a finger and ended the world?

Me: "Can we just put our shoes on?"

It's not Thursday yet. You have approximately 10,000 requests to make of me between now and Thursday. Why can't we just get out the door? But I didn't say that out loud because I have a filter. See! I have a filter!

Collecting myself, I picked Mars up and sat him on the red chair, a rocker that looks like it was once velvety and red and in my mind still is, despite the repeated yogurt spills and dog drool swipes and dried up toddler slime. It's a comfort spot where Gomez, Mars, and I miraculously fit together and rock and read and talk, on old slime. See also the chapter on keeping a sanitary house with children and what a fiction that is.

“Some religions, like Keevine’s, believe that when you read the stories in The Bible, that everything happened in the story exactly like it says. But that’s not really what we think. We think that the stories are there to talk about and to look for what they really mean. The stories are just stories to get an idea of what we should learn. And when you go to church with Gramma, you guys talk about what the message is in the story. It’s called a moral. So if there’s a story that says Jesus held up one finger and ended the world, they’d talk about how that’s a story and what the story means, what the moral of the story is. And when you want to read stories about God and Jesus, you can do that at church or with me. But let’s not talk about what we believe with Keevine anymore, ok?”

“But Keevine talks about it all the time and then I get scared.”

“I know. So let’s talk about what you can say to Keevine.”

We went over a few quotes he could use to get Keevine to stop talking about scary end-of-the-world stuff and practiced them and Mars felt better and I managed to hold back my seething annoyance at Keevine’s religion. It’s just part of multiculturalism. The downside, obviously, but part of it.

Rob: "That went a lot better than it would have if I'd talked to him. I was just going to tell him Keevine's full of shit."

By the time I wrapped up this conversation, I was beat. So that meant that Rob got the next fun conversation after an incident just a few minutes later. I turned around and saw Mars waving his penis around (something Gomez was getting in trouble for and now I knew why) and I caught the word "vagina."

"You're up." I said to Rob, and went into my bedroom and shut the door to binge watch Netflix. Rob took Mars downstairs to have a little chat.

Rob came up a short time later to report on his conversation with Mars. It went something like this.

"I told him to keep it in his pants. He told me that he was just pretending to pee red. He showed me with red playdough which he threw while miming peeing red. To his credit, he kept it in his pants while he mimed."

I have no idea what the word "vagina" had to do with that. And I'm letting that one go. Because you can't win them all. Or any of them where this obnoxious kid in Mars' class is concerned, apparently. If you feel I've made a jump in my attitude toward Keevine, I have and you'll soon see why.

Later, we learned that Mars had *heard* Rob say that Keevine was full of shit because Mars reported on his subsequent playground conversation with Keevine.

"When Keevine started talking about the end of the world, I told him my dad says he's full of shit but Keevine said 'no way. I'm *the* shit. You're *dad's* full of shit.'"

So no matter how awkward the conversation, or how well you think you handled it, apparently the lesson here is that you'll get to try again.

This turned out to be true many times over. I heard more concern later. More about the New World and how Mars wasn't ready and would die. I hated this. I also had lunch with Keevine and then followed the kids to the playground where I witnessed Keevine, moments before polite as pie, calling a kid a "bitch" and I swear, I've never heard such a young kid *spit* a word. His lips were positively plosive as he spit that word across the playground. He was threatening kids and leading a gang about some slight that had happened. This was clearly a frequent occurrence. The kids on the playground definitely knew Keevine's role of boss.

Then there were days when Mars didn't want to go to school because Keevine and he weren't getting along. He'd be throwing fit after fit and finally he and I would be on the way to the bus stop and I'd ask "Mars, how big is your worry?"

And that's when he'd tell me that he was scared about Keevine.

Worst of all was the day a friend called me one morning before school to tell me about the game Keevine and Mars had been playing and how her daughter had ended up in the middle.

My mom friend said, "So this is awkward but my daughter just told me she's afraid to go to school because she's afraid Keevine and Mars are going to grab her and punch her and she doesn't feel safe. I told her I'd text you and we could set up a playdate because Mars is her friend and she doesn't need to be scared of him."

Did I mention this friend is a lawyer? Remember how my husband helps protect victims? Why was my kid involved in something where some kid was threatening to punch a little kindergarten girl who has a lawyer for a mom? Dangit!

I immediately went to Mars. "Mars, is there a reason why she's afraid of you and Keevine?"

Mars avoided my gaze but eventually came out with this. "Keevine's been making me play this game where we capture the girls. He always wants me to go get her and yesterday he punched her in the stomach."

"Oh my! No wonder why she's scared. You know that's not okay, right? It's not okay for your friend to be afraid of you. You can't do what Keevine wants if he chooses to play like this." I could feel my anger rising and tried to reel it in. I didn't want him to be scared by my attitude but my words began speeding up. "What can you do instead of capturing the girl for Keevine?"

"Tell a teacher."

"That's right. Because it's not okay for our friends to feel scared at school. She especially shouldn't be scared of *you*. You should be there to help your friend."

I texted my friend my apologies and what I'd learned and we had a chat about Keevine and my concerns about him. I called the school that day and complained and told them what Mars had told me about the game they were playing. I questioned why the playground staff weren't more involved in helping such young kids learn to behave and play appropriately on the playground. My friend understood and also called the school with her concerns.

We worked through it all, all school year long.

And then, ahhh…summer. I thought we were done. I was done hearing about Keevine for the summer, tra la, tra la! But then Mars pulled this one out after school had been out for about a month.

"Keevine was being controlled by the man-on-fire-who-lives-under-the-earth-and-hates-Jesus and he punched me in the stomach."

And it made me understand why people send their kids to private school. Setting aside your annoyance at someone else's religion is apparently the line you cross from acceptance over to tolerance, if you can make it that far. On the one side, you accept and see the good in the view of another. This is acceptance. On the other side of the line, you scream through clenched teeth, "I'll stab someone at the school if they put that kid your class next year."

It is now mid-summer. If not for this book, I would have nearly forgotten about Keevine in the bliss of warm days at the park and late evenings eating frozen yogurt. Recently, Mars and Gomez and I were sitting in the red chair killing time by snuggling and joking before heading to see a community play.

Mars suddenly grabbed my cheeks and looked at me. "I picture you in heaven with Jesus and there's a pool and…"

Then Gomez grabbed my cheeks and turned my face to him. "Mom, you and Jesus have a contest to see who can throw you into the pool!" To reiterate, Jesus is throwing me into a swimming pool in my child's religious view. How's that New World for you?

Mars, laughed with abandon and recalled the detail "with your clothes on."

I leaned back and rocked the chair, open throat laughing. "So Jesus and I are having a contest to see who can push each other into the pool with our clothes on? Oh good."

Gomez interrupted to clarify, "No, THROW each other into the pool!"

I squeezed them each in my arms and kissed Gomez's head.

Mars then added, "When you go to heaven, you stay the same age as you were when you died."

I remarked, "Oh yeah? I'm planning on making it to 100 so I hope not."

"Why?" Mars asked.

"Because," I answered, "I plan to live to 100 but your body doesn't work as well at 100 as it did before. I'd want to be a bit younger so my body would work better again."

I'm betting Jesus throws harder than 100-year-old me.

This chapter was brought to you by public school, Keevine, the Letter F, the number 666, and mostly Jesus, holybehisname, who would push me - nay, THROW me - into a pool when I'm 100 years old. Holy crap, the challenges of parenthood don't stop with gross stuff. They continue all the way into school days and beyond.

While on vacation when Gomez was two, I took a picture of him with a rock over his eye. At least it wasn't in his mouth. Just before the picture, he was on Rob's shoulders and I said, "Gomez what are you eating?" and he got a big grin and pulled a rock out of his mouth.
This habit hasn't gone away either. At 3 ½, I asked him what he had in his mouth because I heard loud crunching at bedtime, and he had an orange, crayon-crumble covered tongue.

Chapter 28

What's in the Bag?

"When was the last time you looked in that bag?"

One day when I picked my three-year-old up at daycare, my daycare lady chastised Rob and me about the contents of the bag we send with our son. This was completely unfounded. That bag must have all the things she needed, surely. It'd been unopened for a month. So the things that were useful a month ago should all still be in there, right? Right?

Daycare lady: "Do you know what's in there? Because there were no pairs of underwear, about three winter coats, five pairs of socks... do you have any socks left at your house?--and no changes of clothes."

I laughed maniacally and swore that we had it all together as I rushed out her door to our car.

This is what happens when the only person to do anything with the bag is the three-year-old, who, it appears, has slowly added things to it. Meanwhile, the adults have not added anything nor taken anything out, apparently.

I checked out the contents when the kids and I got home. Here was what was in there:

Four pairs of socks, two coats, a superman book, a keychain, a Lego guy, a pair of underpants. 0 shorts or pants, 0 shirts, 0 hats.

She was wrong, we do have socks at home (now).

While sitting on the floor of the living room, folding the last bits of laundry that evening (as if I've ever seen the last bits of laundry. That'll be the day.) Mars and I had this conversation about girls.

"You know how they do this?" He mimed a girl tucking hair behind one ear and a smile timidly took over his face.

I nodded. "Yeah."

He grinned. "I feel funny when they do that."

Smiling had now completely overwhelmed him and a new look I'd never seen before crossed his face: embarrassment? No. More like a post-flirty combination of confused and bewitched.

I promptly fell into a fit of laughter on the floor.

Mars' ears turned red and he asked, "What?"

I sat up. "You like them, don't you? The girls that tuck their hair behind their ears?"

Mars snorted and replied, "Yeah. Why are you laughing?"

I laid a sock down. "No, it's nothing, I just think you're going to marry a girl." I then grabbed another sock and put it in the pile of unmatched socks and Mars ran, thudding all the way up the stairs.

I finished up and came upstairs and started cleaning up there.

"Mars, did you do your afternoon routine?"

"Agh!!" He growled loudly and picked up his backpack and slammed it on the floor. "If I do my routine, can we watch 'Cake by the Ocean, original version'?"

"Do your routine," I tossed a shoe over to the closet.

"Can you go on Youtube and type in the search box "Cake by the Ocean, original version"?"

"Mars, put your shoes in the closet. Otherwise, you won't know where they are and you'll be late in the morning."

"Agh, Fine! Then, can you go on Youtube and type in the search box 'Cake by the Ocean, original version'?"

He probably repeated this five times. "Cake by the Ocean, original version."

Rob called out from the kitchen, where he was cooking dinner.

"Wait, what was it again? Crumpets by the Seaside? A remix?"

"No, it was Pie by the Creek." I grabbed Mars' shoulder and pointed. "Shoes."

Mars, patiently for once, completely missing the teasing said, "No, no, no. It's 'Cake by the Ocean, original version'."

Rob: "Salad Tongs on the Sand?"

Me: "No, not sweet enough. 'Cobbler at the Pond'."

Rob: "Ice Cream at the Inlet."

Mars: You guys are assholes.

Well, that's what he should have said. He didn't. He waited patiently until we finally *typed it in the search box* as he'd instructed and his video came on. By then, Rob came into the living room and Gomez was there too.

As we started watching it, Mars' eyes got huge because of all the girls in bikinis in the video. There is also a giant cake in the video, and he was excitedly anticipating that apparently, there is a lot of throwing of the cake by the girls in bikinis and he liked that idea. A lot.

We turned off 'Danish by the River' when Gomez asked, "Are they saying the f-word?"

In case you didn't know, the song Cake by the Ocean has a bunch of the f-word in it. My five-year-old asked to see the video, it turned out, because some kid at school told him about the girls in the bikinis and Mars thought this sounded marvelous. I doubt that he cared about the f-word part.

"Let's get your reading done while Dad finishes dinner."

Mars, Gomez, and I headed to the red chair with a pile of books.

Me, smelling something minty on Gomez's breath as he snuggled into my lap: "Gomez, are you eating something?"

He shook his head vigorously.

Getting caught isn't all that abnormal for him. On a recent camping trip, he was eating restaurant crayons during story time in the tent and nearly bit me as I struggled to get him to spit out the pieces. He eats crayons often.

"Gomez, what are you eating?"

Gomez: "I don't want to tell you."

Me: "Just tell me the truth. If you're honest, you won't be in trouble."

Gomez, more emphatically and whining: "I don't want to tell y-you!" (voice shaking)

Me: "Did you eat candy?"

Gomez: "No"

Me, thinking: "Did you get ahold of some gum?"

Gomez: "No."

Me: "Just tell me what you ate."

Gomez: "I don't want to."

Me, looking down at chapstick and remembering that he asked yesterday whether chapstick was minty: "Is it chapstick?"

Gomez: "I don't want to tell you!!!"

Rob, laughing: "You said to tell the truth and technically, he's not lying."

I took the half-eaten chapstick away and put it on the tomorrow shelf. The kids hate the tomorrow shelf above all other punishments in the house. I put things on that shelf and forget them for a lot of tomorrows. I mean to give it back tomorrow but if no one asks, I forget. And even if they do ask for it back, they tend to ask at the same time as I'm in the shower or making coffee or we're about to walk out the door OR at the same time as they're asking for four other things. So it doesn't always happen and then there the item sits, getting swallowed by piles of clothes on my shelf.

Gomez has been known to try to figure out when tomorrow is which quickly becomes a more complicated and esoteric conversation than you'd think.

Gomez: "Is it tomorrow yet?"

Me: "Nope."

Gomez: "Is it tomorrow the day after this night?"

Me: "Yes."

Gomez, the next day: "Is it tomorrow now?"

Me "technically, it will never be tomorrow."

Gomez wails in despair. The tomorrow shelf never comes.

Screaming ensued about the mostly-eaten minty chapstick on the tomorrow shelf. Then, at dinner he flatly refused to try any of the food because "it's yucky." Yeah, stir fry is yucky, but chapstick and crayons are delicious.

The following morning, Rob found a box of graham crackers in Gomez's bed. He's a squirrel, apparently. He'll eat things he squirrels away for himself but nothing I make.

This was a total of 12 hours of our lives. It's like this every. Glorious. Day. Welcome to school aged kids and all that comes with that. It's just a new twist on the Stop Licking That conversation. Stop eating chapstick. No, you can't sing the f-word and watch girls throw cake in bikinis, now finally put your shoes in the closet and eat your danged dinner.

Chapter 29

Twenty-One Things I Lost, Forgot, or Got Wrong Before 9 a.m.

The beginning of Summer:

1. I forgot the paperwork for the first day of camp at work so had to stop by my office and get it.

2. Said paperwork was blank because I had forgotten to fill it out on Friday or all weekend while it sat forgotten at work.

3. I forgot a pen to fill it in when I left the office.

4. I forgot my purse at home which contains pens that I could have used.

5. I forgot my son's jacket in case it rains.

6. I forgot to put sunscreen on my son in case it doesn't rain.

7. I forgot to bring sunscreen for them to put on my son (who is clear, like me and needs constant sunscreen slathering).

8. I forgot a hat for him.

9. Over the weekend I lost every plastic bag, paper bag, and both kids' lunchboxes. I put the kids lunches in a bagel bag and a hospital bag with "Steve" on it.

10. On Sunday when my husband went grocery shopping, he forgot the grocery list in the car so he forgot to buy Ziploc bags and we completely ran out of those too. So the inside of the kids' lunches looks a lot like the outsides. Thanks, Steve.

11. I forgot a water bottle for my son's camp.

-1 so back to 10. I found a water bottle in the car so we'll call that one a win!

11. But back to 11 because I forgot to wash it and have no idea when it was washed last because it's a forgotten-in-the-car water bottle but I did remember to have my son refill it from the water fountain and that's definitely clean so we'll let that one go now.

12. I forgot my husband's cell phone number. Okay, that's a lie. I don't actually have it memorized. Also, I'm going to be out of town for the rest of the week so his is the actual number they *need*. I think I might remember it correctly 10% of the time. There's only like 2 digits I'm unsure of but if they're wrong I'm sure it won't work for calling him. Obviously the probable wrong number is a problem on the form I filled out. Or maybe this was the 10% chance and I got his number right. Fingers crossed.

13. In the paperwork at home there was a list of acceptable and unacceptable "Take Apart" items for this camp. All the normal parents brought a broken DVD player or a broken CD player. Meanwhile, I brought the motor from our broken ceiling fan. It's so weird that it didn't make either the acceptable or the unacceptable part of the list. So I don't actually know if I messed up or not but it looked weird and my kid can hardly carry the stinkin' thing so probably this was a screw up. Or maybe he'll pull it off with moxie. That kid oozes with moxie. Except when he's nervous. Like he was this morning when I screwed up our entire morning. And probably his life.

14. At sign in, I found out that they forgot to add my son to the list despite the fact that I signed up and paid for this camp in March. I know this is not actually my fault but I then forgot how I registered him and got so flustered that I'm sure this somehow gets categorized as me getting *something* wrong.

15. Then on my way out after abandoning my terrified, possibly unwelcome child at camp with a jenky lunch and the wrong Take Apart item, I heard the ladies who were checking people in asking each other

if something from a story sounded believable. And maybe that didn't have anything to do with me but I was worried that they didn't believe me. Even though I definitely paid for and registered him for this camp. And my paranoid reaction is probably something I got wrong.

16.Then I started thinking about how I'm wearing a ridiculous skirt and t-shirt combo because they're so comfortable and I realized that everything about my clothes is wrong. My skirt has this hole in it that I always think I'm going to sew. So after I wear it, I set it aside as though I'm going to do that but then

17. I forget to sew it and then I get annoyed that it's out so I put it back on the shelf. And then

18. I re-forget that it's got a hole in it and only remember that it's super comfy and have this dumb idea that if I wear a skirt, that's getting dressed professionally-ish enough even though the only long summer skirts I own are the kind that can actually double as pajamas.

19. So I rush home because the lady who forgot to list my son on the sign in asked if she could call me in an hour. Because that's how long it takes to figure out if I'm a whackadoodle in a ripped pajama skirt t-shirt combo that's trying to sneak my kid into a camp or an actual on-top-of-it-for-one-single-moment-mom because I signed him up in MARCH but I knew I'd forgotten my cell phone so I'd better get home so she could call me.

20. But then I realized when I got home and looked in my purse that my phone wasn't there. It was in the pocket of my robe and I'm basically a ninja because I found it without my husband calling it.

21. I forgot to mention my other son. I definitely don't have the mental capacity now to figure out what I forgot, lost, or screwed up there. I'm sure he's walking around with boogers on his dirty face but at least he's got Steve's hospital bag full of lunch and probably clothes on. Probably.

"Innapropriate comments? That's what little girls are made of."

"Little girls are made of Adderall."

-Conversation with Snotrocket Kelley

Chapter 30

Three Inventions That Would Make Me the World's Best Mom

Sometimes I'm an awesome parent. I have incredible moments. When they happen, it's like having a cape and a world's greatest mom award all at once. I got it right! I got it right! "I'd like to thank the Academy…"

My mother-in-law tells me I'm doing just fine and my sister-in-law sends me a text telling me I'm pretty for no reason at all. My husband talks about how the kids want to be with me and how he's basically a consolation prize when it's his turn to do bedtime. And then I go write in my room alone, satisfied with the glory of parenthood. Then my husband makes it even better because just as I've finished writing the perfect chapter, he whooshes into the room and says "come look at this."

I follow him and he hands me our younger son wrapped in a cerulean towel. "What on—" I start to ask.

He answers, "—just come here."

He's pulled our five-year-old from the bath as well. Mars is in a yellow towel the color of a kindergarten crayon and I stand with him against my hip, holding a wet Gomez. Mars points out away from the deck.

And there is a double-banded, brilliant rainbow. We stood there for so long, the drizzle abated and our toes got wet on the deck but we didn't care. I just soaked up the view and the pause it gave me to hold my kids and hold this moment. If only we could hold these moments in our hands.

This was my favorite thing that happened that summer. But these moments are rare, really rare, and they are fleeting. So often, I notice the times when the kids have taken turns crying for the entire morning and then after an hour of that crap, I let slip the comment "oh my God, kill me now." Yup, that also really happened. I'm glad that one can slip away and I'm not forced to hold it and carry it around with me.

Of course I regretted it immediately. The Academy ripped the award from my hands. And worse than the lost award, I knew immediately that the phrase will be repeated. And "oh God, kill me now" out of a five-year-old's mouth is more than lamentable; it's terrible.

But since there are these incredible moments with rainbows, I think, "We can do it. We can be awesome. We can be the best family EVER. All the time. Always. Every Minute."

But we'd need some help. We'd have to set reality aside for a moment. Force it out of the way and make a new reality in which we are awesome. Always. All the time. Every minute.

Here are the three inventions that would make us all the best parents ever and mean that I never, ever hear my five-year -old say "kill me now."

The 30 second retractor.

This invention would help me solve the problem of letting a dumb thing come out of my mouth, like when you ask a rhetorical question of your kid like this.

"It's time to go. Do you want to put your shoes on?"

It doesn't matter if he wants to put his shoes on. A good question I *could* have asked was "do you want to wear tennis shoes or rain boots?" The 30 second retractor would help because it would take me back 30 seconds so I could ask the right question.

This would also help when you lose your temper or when you say "What in the actual EFF" to your child, which I haven't done but I have said "shut up" and that's nearly as bad. I feel like complete junk about it. So, if I had a retractor button, I could take that back.

Scene: Kids in the morning alternate crying for 45 minutes and miraculously have eaten and have passably clean clothes on. I'm sweating and don't know what day it is. I haven't showered or gotten dressed but I am giving up and going to work in my pajamas. I slept in a work t-shirt so that's sort of like getting dressed for a job. Hmmm…sort of.

Just as I shuffle both kids out the door, the younger one says, "*I* wanted to go out the door first." He throws himself on the mercy of the doorstep in a meltdown. The older one says, "I'm an asshole so I'm going to rub it in right now that *I'm* the first one out the door." Okay, he doesn't say that. He just goes, "You can't be the first one out the door because *I* am."

"SHUT UP, you." I point. "YOU, Get in the car!"

Horrible, right? Kind of normal, but nonetheless sucky. But with the 30 second retractor, I could take back that "shut up," and not have yelled "Get in the car!"

With those 30 seconds back, I'd have scooped up three-year-old, Gomez, lovingly *smooch, smooch* and offered him a choice: walk out before me or I'll carry you!

(Aside, I got in trouble with my childcare provider for carrying Gomez too much. I don't care. He has the plumpest most kissable cheeks in the whole world and he's my last baby and I'll carry him until I throw my back out. So there.)

Back to rainbows and being magical parents because…the retractor.

Suspended animation

This invention would give me a chance to press pause on my little people. You should be able to put your little beans into suspended animation once a week for up to an hour. It would work like sick time where if you didn't need it, then you could accrue the hour from one week and add it to the next week. That way if you get effing diarrhea and can't help a trip to the bathroom, and *also* need to supervise your children who are likely to do cool things like take all their clothes off and go out the front door to jump in puddles in the driveway naked, you could stop nonsense in its tracks. I could've used this when I was about to lose my mind in the middle of the night. I also could have pushed the pause button and used the suspended animation feature on the toddler who had just stuck his finger in his own asshole and turned himself into a human poop piñata all over the upstairs bathroom. I could have used it to yak. You can't give us parents too much time though. Have you seen what we do with handing our phones over to our kids? We can't handle an endless supply of this parenting-saving invention. We'd overuse it. Although in fairness, I'm not sure 60 minutes would be enough. But hopefully one hour a week would occasionally accrue to be just the amount I need. But it definitely needs to accrue. Otherwise, I'd get to the end of the week and if I hadn't used my hour, I could take a really long shower or have sex. It has to accrue though. Otherwise, it'd be lame like fuel points where I just forget about them and then it's the 2nd of the month and I realize the gas tank is almost empty and I'm like "crap, 450 fuel points just expired." Only it'd be worse because it would be lost suspended animation time. So it'd accrue and I'd be able to throw up if I needed to or deal with broken glass without the added fun of any meltdowns. Or if I accrued some time, I'd just have a reminder of what single life was like.

A prehensile tail

Humans are weird, tail-less, nearly bald animals compared to other mammals. I bet the real reason dogs and cats like us is that they feel sorry for us. I bet they're all, "Oh those poor weird-looking balding things need love and probably warmth. I'll be the Jesus of the animal kingdom and snuggle them and keep them warm at night even though they feed me that terrible food that stinks up the entire city of Denver when Purina's factory is actively manufacturing it." I may have gotten slightly off track here, but I'll bring it back eventually.

The best of the monkeys can swing by their tails. Dog tails just knock stuff off of coffee tables and cats' tails exist only to tickle your nose when you're trying to ignore the cat and finish your book while meanwhile she's trying to make you pet her. Cats' tails are for balance and annoying their pathetic, mostly-bald caretaker animals, but they can't control their tails or use them to pick stuff up. This is why my invention is the *prehensile* tail. You can control a prehensile tail and use it on purpose. Mothers would sprout the prehensile tail during the 2nd trimester of pregnancy which is the only one that doesn't suck that bad. You're not second guessing every food choice or puking and you still have enough energy to touch your toes. Congratulations! You get a tail to help your parenting awesomeness.

The prehensile tail can be used to open the door when you're holding a car seat in one hand and a toddler in the other. It can be used to reach into the back seat and hand out snacks, or separate the unruly children. It has so many uses, I can't believe we haven't sprouted them already.

As the mother stops nursing, she then has the option to shed her tail or to keep it. It's a tricky choice because as mothers, we're attached to our pre-pregnancy image of ourselves, which persists in pictures but is otherwise seemingly a figment of our imaginations. We all need to let that image go. We are not that woman anymore. We're attached to this image of our bodies before the tail sprouted, but the tail… I mean who can do without once you have it? Plus, you'd have to patch the tail hole in your pants. I don't know about you, but I'm still wearing nursing bras because they're comfy all around and I haven't nursed in two years. So I'm betting utility would win for me and I'd keep the tail. Still, a discussion among women would occur about the choice. I can imagine women sitting around counseling a young mother on the decision.

"I got rid of mine. Worst mistake I ever made. I keep forgetting and wearing my tail yoga pants and that's embarrassing. Plus, yesterday Midge and Yotis, my kids, were fighting in the backseat and I wished for my tail so much. But they just kept screaming 'Mine' and 'Mom, he's touching me'. If I'd had my tail, I could totally have stopped their fight. But there I was with nothing to do about it but turn the music up. Sure I guess, I could ignore them or pull over and deal with them. Blech. Don't do it. Keep the tail."

And a bevy of other women would cluck their tongues and nod in agreement. One would pick up her tea with her tail and feel guilty for having drawn attention to her smart decision on the matter in front of the poor lamentable woman who had ditched hers.

A third woman would agree. "Keep the tail. I used mine just yesterday to make a margarita while doing the laundry. I'm invincible with this tail. Seriously, I don't miss my pretail leggings one bit. Keep it."

The woman who made the regrettable decision to give up her tail would choke back tears while admitting, "I'm trying to talk Martin into a 3rd child so I can get the tail back. I know, I know. That means a minivan and being outnumbered, but I don't know what else to do." And she'd slump over in sobs while all the other women patted her on the back with their tails. I'd be behind them, holding the scepter of invented perfect parenting in my tail.

SCEPTER!

"Can we just agree to declare the argument "and I turned out fine," to be null and void?

Chapter 31

My Book's Not Funny

The book I wrote before this one (*Between Families*, if you're interested) is a serious story where you get sucked into the life of the protagonist and want nothing more than to pull her out of the story and hold her, give her a nice warm cup of honey and milk, and tuck her into a safe life where nothing can hurt her again. While a compelling story, it is decidedly not funny.

And the reaction of one of my coworkers made that painfully clear. I am funny. My book is not funny. And so began the joke about how I should write a book that *is* funny. This book is my attempt at that but this is a little break from that attempt.

I am funn

y. This part is not.

Parenting is not all jokes. Yes, they help, but there's a point at which you have to be honest that jokes and tricks and you as parent alone are not cutting it and you need to get bigger better help.

I've mentioned that my kids are pretty different from one another. With Gomez, the tricks and jokes have worked. But with Mars they didn't. Well, they were better than nothing but it was a constant struggle to figure out how to deal.

Mars battles. He transforms his soul to screams and hurls them at you. And he does not give up. Ever. I have never seen him wear himself out from his tantrumming which, when he was younger, was almost entirely verbal. I get triggered by volume but I didn't know that when Mars was younger. I only knew that I would get extremely frustrated, put him in a timeout, he'd scream and bang against the door with all his might and keep screaming, and I'd try to keep him away from me while I calmed down and figured out what to do. Then after the two minutes that corresponded with his age and so were the number of minutes I was supposed to leave him, I wouldn't really be calm yet. He'd have been screaming at me the entire time. But I'd think it had been the right number of minutes and not want him to feel abandoned and so I'd go back in and try again. The whole thing would start all over again. It didn't help either of us in our efforts at calming.

Mars started throwing wild fits when he was about 16 months old where he'd laugh in this really out-of-control way and run out of any timeout. I believe I mentioned his difficulties with peeing on things when he was mad. Those subsided, but the throwing his head back, launching his voice into the world and having unrelenting screamfests lasted and lasted. We tried sticker charts for him, sticker charts for me, sticker charts for both of us, timers, coping strategies like blowing up pretend balloons and ripping up paper. We tried guided visualization. He and I tried these tapping videos that direct you to strategically tap on your forehead to help with anger and frustration.

But it didn't matter; we'd end up back in it together again. I'd tell him to take a break, he'd scream at me, throw things, and scream some more. I'd carry him to his room. He'd bang and scream. I'd walk away. He'd slam things and scream more. I'd cover my ears and breathe and try to calm down before going back to him. It would not be enough time and I'd go back in and end up screaming back at him. We did this dance for at least two years.

At one point, despite having worked as a professional in child welfare, despite having warned parents against it for exactly these reasons, despite having a firm value system that denounces this exact thing, I spanked Mars.

This continues to be a tremendous source of shame for me and I think that my guilt about it is justified. It was not the right thing. It was not one incident. I spanked Mars a few times. And the last time was particularly bad.

Before spanking, I had tried and tried calming strategies that I do now as well. I had tried having Mars ball up his fists and squeeze imaginary lemons. We'd blown up imaginary balloons to encourage deep breathing. I'd tried time-ins where I stayed with him and tried to get him to mimic my breathing. I can honestly say these were good seeds to plant for the future, but they did not work.

I don't recall the details of why I ended up spanking Mars that last time. If I had to guess I'd say I was probably sleep deprived and he had probably had many, many tantrums over the course of several days before we got where we ended up. I do remember the snap where my mind cracked wide open and I had these lying thoughts. The thoughts were terrible; they told me insanity, like that he needed to *feel* the spank. It's even more horrifying to type than it is to even let myself remember this. And this was the exact thing I'd warned parents about. You might go too far.

Immediately after it was over, I knew how terrified he was and what a horrible thing I'd done. I shook and walked away, terrorized at what I'd done.

"It hurts, Mom."

I was so upset, the memories of it are all jumbled together and I can't even remember which thing happened when. I remember being terrified that I'd left a mark and what might come from that. I remember wondering whether I should keep Mars out of school if he did have a mark. But then I thought that if I did that, I was isolating him and that child welfare would look at that as scarier than if he were just spanked. I remember thinking my career was over and I deserved it. *I* deserved it, but if my husband were a single parent because he did the right thing which was to send me far, far away from my children, how would I make any money to send child support? I went so, so far ahead of myself.

"Rob, you should kick me out. You should leave me."

Marks are the legal line Colorado draws between spanking and abuse. It would turn out, I hadn't left any. Mars was fine. But legal line or no, I'd made a terrible mistake, and one I could not take back. I had to learn from it. I *had* to do something different.

I couldn't sleep or eat and had diarrhea for days.

I have a degree in education. I have experience teaching extremely traumatized students. I once had a student who was so traumatized her pupils dilated and her face turned flat while the real *her* disappeared and she tore a closet door off its hinges and hit me with it before I could get out of the way. I literally have scars to prove it. I have had students like this and worse, and I have never lost it in those scenarios. I know what to do in crisis. I know how to calm my face first, and breathe, and I know to scan my body for tensions and release them before having any reaction. I thought knowing that, having those experiences would protect me from ever making a mistake like I did with Mars. I truly thought my background and knowledge would make me the best, most perfect parent ever. But that's not real life and all my background and experience weren't enough.

Thankfully, Mars was fine. Eventually I was too. I had my husband and my mother to talk to about it. My husband reminded me of what a tough kid Mars is and talked about solutions. I don't remember what all he said but he didn't choose that immediate moment to tell me I was a good mom, which was good, because I absolutely couldn't hear it right then. I think he told me I'm too hard on myself. He shrugged and said it was okay and he loved me. I bawled to Gomez's childcare provider who told me "Karin, it's going to be fine." She also warned me I'd likely make more mistakes and told me not to be so hard on myself. None of the people I shared my terrible mistake with hated me or shamed me or even had trouble understanding the situation.

I sat Mars down and told him through tears that that would never happen again and it hasn't. We put Mars in play therapy and that was the final tool that helped him access all the things we'd been trying to teach him about breathing and keeping his voice at a reasonable level instead of yelling all the time. It was the thing that finally got him to take breaks and to *take* them as breaks instead of as punishment and use them to calm down. We developed a calming kit for him to use and he began using it. We'd been developing those skills with him for years and they never took until he finally went to play therapy.

So as much as there are tricks and tips in parenting books and there are funny anecdotes and stories, and there's knowledge of child development, and all of those things go into making a parent prepared and ready to handle their kids. As much as that's all true, none of us are perfect. No one knows all the ways to help and no parent should do it alone. Sometimes, it's not at all funny. Sometimes it's horrible and terrifying and you need help. I know I did. And I'm really glad we got it for Mars during Kindergarten.

Mars (3) one morning when we were snuggling in bed said, "How are we going to eat any breakfast when we're doing all this happiness?" How indeed.

Chapter 32

The Best Parts of Parenting, and an Apology to my Children for Writing This, Sort of

I love so many things about parenting. I love watching my children, the people I know better than anyone I've ever met, the people who have seen more of the good the bad and the ugly of me than anyone I've ever known, my absolute favorite people I've ever met in this world! I love watching them learn something new. I love watching my son learn to get on a ski lift himself or skip for the first time or ride a pedal bike without training wheels. I love driving in the car and having Gomez ask too quietly and too quietly and then finally YELL that he wants the radio louder and how we all drive along singing our hearts out. I love hearing about Mars' day. I'm honored to be this intimately close with the inner workings of someone's mind when my son tells me for the first time he's afraid of dying.

I love the moments in parenting. It's full of moments, this life. I especially cherish the quiet ones when I've tucked my kids into clean sheets, with their fingernails cut and their hair freshly washed. I love when they've cuddled into the same bed with each other and their eyelashes extend into a galaxy of plump-cheeked serenity. There has been the bliss of a string of moments. Not every moment is bliss, but there are so, so many that are. The moments are a hue I can't describe, like they've been pearled and possess a glow that evades when you try to pin it down with description. Life is nothing but a string of moments that we try to pattern into a necklace. And I want my mommy necklace to have order and be wonderful and real. And that includes a lot of humor and honesty and some failure. Also, boogers. I wanted to make a book about that. And certainly, I've shared honestly about the chaos and the joy, the jokes and the disgust, and of course the sheer challenge of it all.

I've included a lot about my kids here. But truly a book is written by a writer, and so it is always, no matter the original intent, about the author. I wrote about me. This book is about how hard parenting is for *me* and how important it is to me.

My favorite thing about me after kids vs. me before I had kids is the shift in my enjoyment of the world from the grand to the small. Where I used to look for a vacation that gave me an expansive vista, a great tale of adventure zip-lining across volcanoes, now I want one where there's a park the kids will like with swings that send you to the sky but don't dump you out on cigarette butts. I want a good back country trail that they'll be able to hike themselves. I want to be somewhere outdoors that won't be too busy for them to take their clothes off and play naked if they want to without being in anyone's way. Where I used to want to hike to the top of a mountain, and the destination, the summit was the goal, now…now I take the kids with a new water filter and we wander a trail as long as we want. We dunk our filter into a stream and collect our own water. We photograph plants and flowers and then look them up on the internet when we get home. When my kids ask how a flower became a fruit, I show them a time lapse video on YouTube that *shows* them how. When there's a puddle and my kids want to put on rain boots and jump in it, I take them out and spend a half hour within a block of our house jumping in the puddles over and over again.

They pull me with tiny arms, to their level to show me the close and the small things I missed all those years I was taking big steps to explore expanses.

I don't do the big stuff as much anymore, but I would say I'm as happy as I've ever been for all the world. I don't get up and go to the gym daily anymore but someone gives me hugs and kisses every day and I pay attention to what they're thinking and learning. My scope narrowed, and that, for me, has made all the difference.

If you've read this far, dear reader, here is the absolute best advice I have about parenting and its evidence is strewn throughout the entire book: enjoy getting to know just exactly who your children are and watch them develop like you are a microscope watching the first unveiling of a rare species, like you are watching the bursting of an entire universe. It will take you apart with it, and if you watch, you will slowly see stars and life and it will grow you into a new human. Probably one with more stretch marks. And if you are my kiddo and you've read this, please know there is nothing in the world more important to me than you. I have really tried my best. I love you and I love being your mom.

If you're mad at me for writing this, well, I get it. But know that I love you so wholly and completely that if I had to die before you were grown, I'd fight through heaven and hell to come back as your dog or cat (even though I know you sometimes forget to feed ours), because the single best thing in my world is snuggling you and comforting you when you cry and making sure you know that I love you. You, my dear boys, are a rare and fascinating species. I'm watching.

P.S. I'm sorry about that one part I wrote. I should have known it would embarrass you. I hope it paid for you to go to college though.

Dear Reader,

A HUGE, ginormous, squeezy-hug kind of THANK YOU for reading *Stop Licking That.* I hope related to something in these pages. And now… did you think you were done? Well, you could be. Or you could read the appendix to find out how useful snot rockets can be. I need help too. So if you like helping, read on.

Writing this book was a huge undertaking. And I'd like it to make it into many people's hands. So, if you either liked or *didn't* like this book, please add a review of your honest opinion to Amazon, Goodreads, and any site that helps readers find books. Readers need to know both why they would and why they would not like this book. Reviews are the single greatest way you can help authors connect with potential readers. Without reviews, books fall lower and lower on the search pages, buried, never to be seen by real readers. And then, writers are sitting there talking to our imaginary friends. And sometimes they lock you up for that. So write a review, recommend this book to a friend, heck, buy a copy for a friend, and help me NOT get locked up for talking to myself!

Also, I like hearing from readers, so please contact me at

Karin@KarinMitchell.com

www.KarinMitchell.com

Www. Stoplickingthat.com

www.facebook.com/karinmitchellauthor/

And if you're interested in reading my serious novel, it's called Between Families. You can get it on Amazon.

APPENDIX
Parenting Tips, Tricks, & Weird Facts

Pregnancy

1. I farted an absurd amount, especially in my first trimester. Some women puke and lose weight; instead, I farted. I was going to be embarrassed about it, but then I farted next to the baby monitor and it was loud enough to turn the thing on, so I decided it was hilarious. Your body releases Relaxin that loosens your joints while pregnant so that the baby can pass through your pelvis. It also means your pubis and sternum might pop like a kids' knuckles in class. Creepy and true. It turns out fine later.
2. There's a point in utero where babies begin dreaming. This was one of the few weekly facts I got that I thought was cool. That's probably also because it was one of the few facts that came without any comparison of the fetus to food. All the comparisons are like, "Your baby's the size of an olive now." "This week your baby is the size of an apple." So they really think pregnant women only know size by food? The dreaming fetus fascinated me. It made me hope the baby had better dreams than me. I dreamt I had to breast feed an anteater. It was terrifying seeing that giant tube nose coming at my boob.
3. Your IQ drops while you're pregnant. It really does. I once went to the wrong car and cried and called my husband to come and get me when it didn't unlock. It was so embarrassing. Making new memories is not really part of life for a while. And by making new memories, I mean you can't remember your gate number when changing planes, no matter how many times you recite C17, it won't stick. Don't worry though, it comes back. Some people told me that it wouldn't. It did. *sticks tongue out at liars*
4. Don't hold your poop in after the baby comes. It's scary to poop after having a baby. I get it. But also, I have a friend who held it for 3 weeks because she was so scared and she filled the toilet and had to call her super to come and deal with it because she couldn't flush it. And that's worse.
5. You might sweat or cry out your hormones after you give birth. Also you may lose hair and have it grow back in all at once so then you have a layer of hair all over your head that's like a half inch long and stands straight up.
6. Some women get pica when they're pregnant. It's a rare disorder (that also has an association with some chromosomal disorders) in which people

want to or do eat inedible things. So women will want to drink gasoline or eat handfuls of dirt. Really does happen. Resolves after pregnancy. Sometimes caused by vitamin or mineral deficiency but not always.

7. Hemorrhoids are varicose veins in your ass. I don't know why, but that makes me laugh.
8. I don't know any science to base this on, but I think you should have a lot of orgasms while pregnant. I think it causes things to contract and that's like free, nearly-effortless exercise that will make you have your baby faster. I think OBs should tell women this and prescribe masturbation. Everyone wins, I bet.
9. Look up Cliteracy. Just trust me. This actually has nothing to do with pregnancy. Or maybe it does…

Infants

1. **Babyproof.** It is totally worth it. Specifically, go beyond the cabinet locks and be sure to watch out for access to second story windows and anchor bookshelves and dressers to the wall. BUT, know that childproofing only gets you so far. Little tiny humans have nothing but time on their hands to figure out how to climb and to drink from the dog bowl. A parable: We had a Plecostomus named Mr. Sticker in our fish tank. He had an unhealthy attachment to a rock in the tank and died. He was so attached to that rock that he literally disintegrated on it. You can't be too attached to control or you'll die stuck to a rock and your baby won't move around at all. You can't control it all. Do what you can, but don't forget to move about the world.
2. **The Baby Trick: Probiotic.** If you have a tiny baby that won't stop crying, (I had one the second time who only stopped crying when I had him wrapped to me while I forcibly held a pacifier in his mouth and bounced on a yoga ball while patting his butt. This is not hyperbole. This was literally what happened) try a probiotic. They make a powdered one that doesn't have lactose in it and for Gomez as a baby it was night and day. With the probiotic we had a wonderful easy-going cherub, without it, he cried inconsolably. Well, unless you wrapped him to you. And patted his butt. And bounced on a yoga ball. And held a pacifier in his mouth.

He was so uncomfortable and then we'd give him some probiotic (I pumped a bottle and put the powder in it and gave him a bottle until he was a tad older and then I just rubbed the dusty stuff on his tongue), and he'd fart a dozen or so times and be happy. He also had baby acne and if we forgot to give him the probiotic, he'd get acne again and then he'd have probiotic and it would go away.

3. **Baby Trick: Time Outside.** If all else fails and you have a crying baby, take the baby outside. No, it's not too cold or too hot. Well, if you live in Florida it might be. Also, I've always wondered this, why do you live in Florida? It looks so very, very hot there.

   (***An aside.** While writing this, I had to put my son's headphones on because a guy at the coffee shop where I was writing was literally yelling at his coworker explaining the types of snakes he's raising and the genetic makeup of how much of which pastel or albino is in the snake. He's selling one "for like, $50. It's a female super pastel." He's talked about super pastels, butter pastels, and albinos. It's desirable to cross a super pastel with an albino. But he'll make you a killer deal if you want to buy a snake. He's against government regulation of snakes, even pythons, despite describing how where he's from (wanna guess where? Yup, Florida) the snake population has gotten so out of control from private citizens buying and growing pythons and then them getting away and living in the wild, that there has been a significant reduction in the number of rodents and small animals. So pet snakes have taken over Florida and are eating alligators and all the small mammals and people are regularly ingesting venom in order to get their bodies to survive a bite. Oh yeah, he talked about ingesting venom too. Want to shop for a snake over a latte? Seriously, why do you live in Florida? It sounds simply awful. This just too weird not to include.* **Aside over**, back to taking babies outside.)

4. Even if it's really cold out, you can get away with a few minutes outdoors. And that may change everything for you and the baby. I remember Mars crying once and not being able to soothe him. Then I started to cry myself which was as much sadness and frustration as it was hormonal. There a lot of hormone shedding on around that time. Which incidentally is a thing. Women build up all these hormones over the course of the

pregnancy and then they have to shed them after it's over. I shed my hormones after my first baby by crying even when I wasn't sad. And I sweat and drooled them out at night after my second baby. Actually, I might just be a drooly sleeper. Okay, I'm definitely a drooly sleeper, but I'll blame a baby. My body's obviously, super-efficient, and makes double use of my drooling to shed hormones.

5. So one time, when I couldn't soothe Mars, a friend was over and he scooped up the baby, and walked right out the door, no shoes or anything. I had been at my wits' end and started crying and fearing for my very ability to maintain my perfect image of my mommy-identity that I'd designed for myself, but which had not yet truly met with reality. This was an early step in dispelling that image. I cried. My friend scooped up Mars and took him outside. I kept crying. Mars stopped though and I realized it was fine. Babies cry. He would be fine. And we all are. As soon as my friend took Mars outside and Mars stopped crying, I could see we'd be okay.
6. I remembered it and have tried to make sure to take my kids outside when they're getting grouchy even now. It works on them, but truth be told, it works even better on me. A good hour or even a whole day outside completely changes me.
7. **Baby Trick: An Empty Plastic Water Bottle.** I used to keep an empty plastic water bottle in my bottom desk drawer for babies. It is hands-down the best toy in the world. No fake crinkly anything is better. An empty water bottle can buy you a solid twenty minutes of entertainment which is really quite a long time for a baby. They love empty plastic bottles. Once they're allowed to eat, they also love an apple core. You can't give your apple core to someone else's baby though, weirdo. You can totally bring an apple on a plane ride or to a movie theater though and letting the baby gum and bite on it can buy you 40 minutes sometimes. Another thing that will keep a baby occupied at the dinner table is a steak bone. These things may be choking hazards though. I don't know. Ask your pediatrician, or read his book instead.
8. **Baby Trick: Seasonings.** Babies also love scents. We forget that all of their senses are new, not just sight and sound. If you've got a fussy baby or just the desire to have the coolest trick up your sleeve, or you're at a

kidless friend's house for dinner, see what seasonings are in their spice rack. Twist the top open a smidge and let the baby smell. It'll plant the seed for interest in foods later and it's fun to watch baby's face animate about new smells. Bonus, potential new baby faces.

9. Baby Fun fact. When mothers kiss their infant's heads, they're ingesting the germs the infant has also taken in. The mother's body uses this to concoct breastmilk specific to inoculating against the pathogens the baby ingests.

Teething

1. Dampen a washcloth with chamomile tea and then put it in the freezer. Let the baby chew on the washcloth.
2. Amber teething necklaces. These probably only make you feel better and make your baby look hippy chic, but whatever. Try it. (Most of the necklaces are made with plastic beads but again, whatever. Try it. Why not?)
3. Give the baby a green onion to chew. If they do it, they'll have breath that will scare off vampires. Wait, I meant to say the onions have a natural analgesic that helps numb the gums. At least supposedly. Plus, no vampires.

Toddlers

Remember the really silly things that your kid did that made you laugh. Do whatever you can to make sure they're easy to access out of your memory bank so that when your kid is acting like a threenager terrorist, you can think of them and keep from losing your mind.

Food

Things I tell myself about them eating, but I can't really accomplish. Still, maybe these'll work for you.

1. Wait until they're hungry. In this world we're living in with no famine (at least where we live,) where you can choose among nine kinds of premade oven potato types in the frozen section, they'll not starve. They'll eat when

they're hungry.

2. Involve kids in the process of gathering the food, making the choices, and preparing meals. I'm not great at this one, because I'm too high strung and I hurry too much, but when I do do it, it really works. Include them in the food process. Have them help choose the food at the grocery store. Make stirfry and let them choose whether you buy green peppers or red, cabbage or water chestnuts, shrimp or chicken. Have them use scissors to cut up the herbs and add them, have them put in the seasonings. Give them a cool plastic toddler knife and something like a banana to cut up and have them serve to everyone.
3. This is a subset of number two but deserves its own category. Dunkers and Plunkers seems to be key in getting them to eat. Give the toddlers a variety of foods chopped up in small bowls and let them choose which things to add into their own dishes. Make a gourd soup from steamed and pureed vegetables mixed with broth. Then give the kids the following as Dunkers and Plunkers: little bowls with sunflower seeds, green onions (which they can cut up with the scissors themselves,) shredded cheese, croutons, sour cream with a spoon, bacon bits, and more. The kids get a bowl of soup and then choose their plunkers to drop in. You can also do dunkers. That's when you have something like breads, crackers, chicken nuggets, and potato slices and have a series of sauces you let the kids dunk their foods into. I have always disliked condiments so it surprised me to try this one but it does work. Dunkers get dunked in sauces, plunkers get dropped into dishes like soups. Kids love dunkers and plunkers. I don't know if it's the name or the involvement, but it works.

Potty Training

1. If your kiddo hides when he or she has to poop, throw poop parties any time anyone poops. Yes, this sounds insane. But not any more insane that crouching under an end table to poop in a diaper instead of in a bathroom. Perspective, you know? And poop parties. Yell "POOP PARTY, POOP PARTY, POOP PARTY, POOP!" and throw you hands around and dance. Or blow a kazoo or whatever. They get over hiding their pooping that way.

2. Never trust a fart. Seriously. Ask Mars.
3. Put a potty in the back of the car, preferably the kind with a lid. Add a diaper to the bottom of it to prevent splashing. Plus, makes for easy cleanup.
4. Put a potty in the kid's bedroom. Yes, you'll occasionally find a potty full of fun but it will help at bedtime with the "But I have to potty" comments.
5. Do the potty dance when they go. I love the potty dance. You make it up. They dance. You dance. Everyone enjoys a good celebration for a job well done.
6. Give the kid this two-choice option "Do you want to pee on my pee? Or do you want me to pee on your pee?" It's less gross if you say "Do you want to go first or do you want me to go first?" But that also doesn't seem to work as well.
7. Keep a handful cheerios in the bathroom and let your kid put one in the potty and then pee on it. I don't know why this works so well but it does. They really like to pee on Cheerios. They get it in the potty then too.

Getting Ready for a 2nd Baby

I had more trouble with the adjustment to the 2nd baby than I did with the first. To prepare for Gomez, we did a lot of things and I'll share the ones that were good.

1. His entire life, we'd referred to things as ours instead of allowing Mars to have them be his. So instead of "mine" we tried for "ours." A lot of kids go through a toddler stage where at the table it becomes "my seat" the house is "my house" the car is "my car". Parents are so stoked to get meaning out of the yips and blabs that come from their kids' mouths, they don't think much about the mine-phase. Or maybe my kid wouldn't have gone through it anyway but I like that we set our household up as an ours and not a mine. This meant Mars wasn't giving up "my room" or "my bottle" or "my car" to his new brother. His whole world wasn't rocked by needing to share everything that had previously been his. He'd already had his world built as a shared place. This may help with jealousy. I don't know for sure but it's worth a shot.
2. Have special toys for your older kiddo that only come out when you have

to do something with the baby like feed or lay the baby down for a nap. The older kid will do something with those things that you didn't think of and that will probably make you want to pull your hair out, but they'll let you get through feeding the baby this way.

3. Rob spent a lot of time having Mars "help" him with the chores of the household and embrace his new role as big brother/helper. He "helped" Rob take 10 minutes to carry the trash 10 feet. He "helped" Rob move the laundry from the washer to the dryer. And thankfully Rob had the patience to take the eternity it takes to have a 2-year-old "help." So before Gomez became interactive, when he was still the blob of a newborn, the adjustment to two kids was awesome with Mars. He bought right into the helper role and had his own toys he used to trash the house with during naps & feedings. But it wasn't to last.
4. So the things that went well with Mars adjusting to having a brother were that he did not seemingly resent his brother. He got a cool tub full of pinto beans which he threw everywhere while I focused on nursing or putting the baby down for a nap. And while it wasn't my favorite thing to clean up, because the carpet in his bedroom was pinto camouflage-colored, he was safe, and entertained, and didn't resent his brother. He also thought of himself as the big (controlling,) helper of our household. So it wasn't all bad. But I don't recommend pushing potty training. I DO recommend poop parties, having lots of pairs of undies on hand and a good sense of humor, also extra time. I also recommend replacing mine with ours. I recall, with all the emotional weight of a mommy, when Mars gave Gomez bite after bite up to and including the very last bite of his cookie at a restaurant. And right on par with that, was the time on the way home from school in the back of the car when Mars was still two and he reached over and held Gomez's baby hand, then said the Lord's Prayer to him.

Winter

1. Duct tape their mittens to their snow suits until they're able to rip duct tape off. You slide their arms through the sleeve and straight into the mitten. Leave the mittens duct taped to the snow suit all the time. It will save you money (not buying replacements) and time (not looking for lost

mittens.)

2. Anytime you wear black thermal underwear, jump around saying "Now is zee time on schprockets ven vee dance!" This has nothing to do with children.
3. Set up an obstacle course indoors using nothing but what you have on hand. For example "Step over the Batman cup, hop on one foot, run down the hall, spin around 3 times on the Sit 'n Spin, touch the door and come back."
4. Search out the biggest snow piles you can find. Encourage the kids to look out for the biggest pile. We spent one winter wearing our snow clothes and climbing the biggest snow piles we could find at the ends of cul-de-sacs and parking lots. It made car trips more fun. My kiddo would be like "HEY MOM! Do you see that pile over there?"

So Tired

On New Year's, celebrate as early as you want. We did Nine Year's Eve. But you can also do Noon Year's Eve. Or They-Can't-Tell-Time-Yet-Anyway's Eve. Netflix has caught on to this because Netflix is brilliant.

Flying with little kids

1. Bring a change of clothes for yourself. I have a former coworker who gave me this advice and my kid totally threw up on me so I was really, really glad I took her advice. You always remember clothes and stuff for the kids, but don't forget them for YOU.
2. Bring a roll of tape, stickers, and an apple. These will buy you time. I know everyone and their brother has an ipad now so maybe you don't need this but I just finally dropped my knock-off Blackberry in a creek and made the switch to a smartphone. Holy cats! Smartphones are handy. Aside over. If your iPad dies or your phone gets dropped in a creek, or your kid's the one in a million who is just not that into screens, or you aren't—stickers, tape, and an apple can buy you a lot of time on a plane with a 6-or-so-month-old to a 2-year-old. And there's a few months there where

they're still legally allowed to sit on your lap but they're too squirmy to…well…anything but be strapped down. And during that time, if you're a normal person who still tries to travel with them on your lap anyway, you might need some tricks up your sleeve.

Holidays

1. At Christmas, here is the milestone you're watching for to be able to tell a kid is ready for you to leave the presents untouched under the tree: he can write to Santa, "I know I have to give all my presents to the thrift store if I open them before it's time." It has to be correctly spelled and punctuated or he's not ready for you to leave the presents out. I learned this the hard way. Twice at least. Don't wrap the presents and leave them out.
2. This is the only Pinteresty thing I've ever done well in my whole life. If you're a Pinterest mom…I unquestionably defer to your superior mom status. And well, we're not the same breed. But you might like this idea: I made a tree on the wall. We had vaulted ceilings and I really wanted a Christmas tree but I knew there was *no way* my kids would leave the ornaments alone. So I got up on a ladder and used garland and lights to make a squiggly Christmas tree. Bonus, you can see ALL of the ornaments and it doesn't take up any space in the living room.
3. OMG, I have another Pinterest thing I do! Maybe I'm craftier than I think. Hey, Pintrest mom, want to hang out? What do you mean I don't know how to spell "Pintrest?" But I was catching up to you. Wait, no, no I wasn't. I still usually wear any craft on my forehead and in my hair. Whatever. Here's my SECOND Pinterest/Pintresty craft thing. I take paper from the recycling bin or more often than not, I use my rough drafts to fold up and cut and make snowflakes. We then tape them to the windows and spray that (probably toxic) fake snow over them and then remove them. This doubles as curtains in my house. Because buying and hanging curtains is hard. And no, there is no way I'm going to make them.

Surgery

If you have a very little kid who has to have surgery, tell the kid that the doctors and nurses are heroes with the power to heal! This makes their masks not so scary and makes your kid willing to walk back to the operating room even if he's only two.

Swearing Substitutions

"Half-Assed" change to "Half-Apple"

"Douche Bag" change to "Juice Bag"

"Douche Canoe" change to "Juice Canoe"

"Motherfucker" change to "Malefactor"

"Holy Shit" change to "Holy Cats!"

"Mother of God" change to "Mother of Pearl"

"Jesus Christ" change to "Cheese and Rice"

FYI, Elsewhere and Assware sound the same out of a toddler's mouth. I have no idea why a child, or anyone really, would say assware.

"Kill me now" change to SILENCE. Shh, just silence, Karin. That one's not a swear. It's just not okay to say.

Having Fun & Playing Games

I love playing and being silly so I do a lot of it in parenting. It's probably the thing I'm best at. So here's a list of some fun things to do with kids.

1. **Batman Says**. Instead of Simon Says, play "Batman Says." It will make you happy. Besides, why are we all listening to Simon, anyway? I know why we listen to Batman. Bonus points if you can do a whole round in a Christian Bale voice.
2. **Paint in a Bag.** Fill a Ziploc with water-based paint. You can put two colors in or just one. You can also add oil. Then tape the bags to a window or sliding glass door and let your toddler play with the bag.
3. **YouTube favorites**. There's the obvious stuff like kittens and bad toddler music videos and pandas. I mean, who can watch a panda video and *not* feel super happy? But my favorite YouTube channel for kids is The Slow Mo Guys. They use slow motion cameras of super high caliber to do fun things like blow up a 6 foot water balloon or to watch paint vibrate on a

speaker or spin a CD fast enough to shatter it. I also love raising kids in the digital age because of how all these kids just stare at screens all the time. Blech, no I don't. I surely do understand it. My kids would NOT be naked in a puddle nor would they wander into the neighbor's house and pilfer their stock of homemade jelly while I cut Rob's hair, if I just did the normal thing and let them watch stuff and play with an iPad. I DO love the digital age for answering questions. My favorite example of this was when Mars asked me how a flower becomes a fruit. I searched YouTube to show him a time lapse video of just that. It's so useful when I remember to use the internets for things like this.

4. **Non-Elimination Musical Chairs**. Instead of taking a chair away every time you stop the music, you can assign point values to the chairs and leave them every time. That way everyone gets to play every time. If you have kids old enough to keep score, they can work on some basic math. If you don't, you can make up the score and the kids will believe you. You could have popsicle sticks for scoring and then have the kids count them but that sounds a little to Pinterest-y for me.
5. **Luchadores 21.** Rob was the one who first started the game where the boys all put underwear on their head and yell "rahhhhrr" and topple into each other.

   Me: "What are you guys doing?"

   Mars: "We're playing Luchadores 21!" He said this with the leg hole of black elastic from a pair of Batman underpants between his teeth.

   Me: "Why 21?"

   Mars: "Because that is the number"

   I half expected du-uh, mom, to come out of his mother. Then he dove back on my husband who picked him up over his head like an actual wrestler and on they went with their game.
6. **Super Valley Girl.** I invented my own superhero to improve all the playing super heroes I have to do because …2 boys. So I invented Super Valley Girl. My brother taught me the overemphatic inflection of the valley girl accent when I was five and I've never forgotten. Mars always wants to play super heroes, so Super valley girl. She says "like" and "totally" a lot. Super Valley Girl like, totally, has the power of AWE-some!

7. **Exercise of Champions.** When Rob was home with the kids on his own in the evenings a lot while I was teaching, he came up with the game "Exercise of Champions." Be prepared to ruin your carpet with this one. Rob took multiple colors of electrical tape and made a track on our carpet. It was in a large L-shape. He used black to make the outlines the width of a beginner's balance beam and then put blue to make rectangles and then toward the ending near some doorways where the kids were likely to go too fast and bonk into doorways and corners, he put yellow to tell them to slow down. So essentially there were 3 zones. He'd have them run for the first zone, then hop for the second, then walk for the third. They loved Exercise of Champions and it got the kids some activity on cold, dark evening winters.

Dealing with Anger—theirs & yours

Teach kids to blow up an imaginary balloon.

To get kids to do deep breathing, teach them to blow snot rockets. Outside only.

Hold them if you can, walk away if you can't. Take breaks without and without the irritating toddler. If you are too irritated, without. If you can hack it, sometimes with is a good idea.

Tear up pieces of paper.

YouTube has these tapping videos that I used to do with Mars. They do help.

Deep breaths, relax your face first, more deep breaths. Sometimes your kiddo will mimic your breathing as you take deep breaths.

Wrestling, and along those lines, I have been known to sandwich my kid between two pillows and bonk him back and forth on my bed. Both kids love this game and it feels like a pretty healthy way to get out your aggression. This is obviously not the thing to do if you're ready to scream obscenities at the top of your lungs though. Don't hurt 'em is all I'm saying.

Smear paint across their grouchy little faces. Water-based paint won't hurt anyone. A bath must follow. Heck, smear the paint on their faces while they take a bath. It made me feel better that one time I did it…

BUT It's not all Games, and It's okay **to get help**. Hard, but the right thing.

I know I talked about it in the chapter, My Book's Not Funny, but I feel like it deserves a spot here too. I made a horrible, horrible mistake with Mars. I don't know that I'll ever get over it. I can't undo it. We needed help and I'm glad we got it. If you find yourself pushing the line of where you thought something was completely unacceptable previously, you should probably get help. Every once in a while, I still talk to our play therapist to check in about things I want to improve on and where I need structured support as a parent. There are some things you can teach your kids and there are other times when it takes a voice that is not yours saying what needs to be said. I wish I had gotten the help sooner. I'm sorry to my son. Truly.

Acknowledgements

Thank you to my husband who supports my writing habit by generally saying, "yes," when I need to go write and by almost never providing any advice about improving my writing. It used to bug me but now I think he's probably right. He's a smart spouse, that man.

Thank you to my brother who I somehow left out of the acknowledgments of my first book, and who continued to support and promote it anyway and never said anything about my forgetting him. Dangit and sorry, and thank you for your support of me and my writing and my boys.

Thank you to my own parents for teaching me that I am first and foremost smart and worth listening to. And I'm sure there were times when they were really sick of listening to me. So I appreciate that. Being listened to was, in my best estimation, the basis for my learning to write. Plus you sell more copies and advocate harder for my writing than anyone else in the world. Thank you for being supportive parents.

Thank you to my sons' teachers and babysitters: Ms. Billings, Mrs. Bartelt- a master teacher if ever there was one, Nature, Evan, Nicole, Ms. Helena, Rocky Mountain Montessori, Ms. Jeny. A special, special thank you to Erica who has taken care of and loved my Gomez since he was a baby and who has let me cry on her shoulder more than once. You made me feel like I could still be a good parent, even when I spanked Mars and I needed to feel like someone cared about ME right then. I can't thank you enough for the love you've so generously bestowed on my family.

Thank you to Laura K Anderson for all her editing. I trust her instincts and it's handy to have someone like that to work with. Also, you're a spectacular teacher and human and I'm grateful to know you.

Thank you to Armen Durunts who designed the graphic The

Disasterlands of Parenthood. Email him requests for other design work at arm.durunts@mail.ru.

Thank you to everyone who read my first book and encouraged me throughout the rollercoaster of publishing a first novel. Thank you again to all the Kickstarter supporters who made it possible. Special thanks to Sammy who read Between Families and then took the time to contact me and tell me that it encouraged her to go to college to become a counselor for kids like Seffra, and THEN went on to contact me at the end of her Freshman year of college. I have a copy of your email on my corkboard to motivate me. There are so many of you who told me about how that book meant something to you. I promise I'll get back to the next volume in the series!

Thank you to Stefanie Post who was the first person I watched read a chapter from Stop Licking That. Watching you read it and laugh/cry was the best motivator for getting this book out! Also thanks to those of you who have sent me pictures of your wadded up clothes in the OB's office. You're my kind of weirdos and I love you.

Thank you to my critiquing group, especially to Kim and Latham who helped me see the need for major structural changes to make the book flow. And thank you to Jason who organizes the group and always gets back to you with thorough feedback that is spot on.

Thank you to the Facebook group, Summit County Moms for being the fastest answer to any mom question you could ever think of and for being a supportive online community. You moms are so stinkin' awesome.

And a GIANT thank you to my mommy tribe friends: Michelle, Emily, Jaci, Kelley, Kristina, Lenka.

Thank you to the following of you referenced in this book: Michelle, Arlie, Maebry, and Steve's hospital bag, Leslie and Sage, Amber Michaelson, Ms. Alice, Erica, Snot Rocket Kelley.

About the Author

I live in Colorado with my husband and two boys where I spend my time teaching, writing, and skiing. I hold a Masters of Writing from Regis University and a Bachelor's in Education from St. Louis University. I love learning and school and kids and fun.

That's the fancy-pants version. Here's the real me. I am afraid of changing lightbulbs. I HATE feet. I hate condiments. I check behind the shower curtain of people's houses because I'm the kind of person who would hide there to scare someone. When I was six I went to school with my coat and no shirt on and made it all day without anyone finding out. When I was ten I didn't brush my hair for four months.

My favorite errand is going to the library. I will pull things out of the trash to recycle them. I love to have conversations about all the things you're not supposed to talk about. I hate country music and jam bands. I have great aim when throwing things especially at other people, but I can't play an upper body sport to save my life. I get competitive about weird stuff like who can spit a watermelon seed farthest. I love life but I get bitchy sometimes. Writing and skiing are my sanity. I speak Swedish and can lick my own elbow. I'm kinda weird.

Made in the USA
Columbia, SC
03 June 2017